7 50

SIGNED

12/23

Vince—

 I hope you enjoy this

story of old Saratoga racing.

It was quite a time

Thank you + Merry Christmas

Michael Veitch

2004

TABLE OF CONTENTS

Introduction .... p.   3

Foundations 1863-1869 .... p.   7

Expansion and Challenge 1870-1890 .... p. 21

Decline and Recovery 1891-1900 .... p. 39

Appendix A. Racing Dates .... p. 55

Appendix B. Trivia .... p. 57

Appendix C. Stakes Histories .... p. 61

Appendix D. Chronology .... p. 91

Notes .... p. 95

Selected Bibliography .... p. 99

Acknowledgements and Credits .... p. 105

About the Author .... Inside Cover

INTRODUCTION

Summer in Saratoga Springs was special for me as a child because it meant visits to the track. My father, Don, would take me to the barn of his uncle, Hall of Fame trainer Sylvester Veitch, to see outstanding C.V. Whitney runners such as Fisherman and Career Boy in the mid-1950's. We saw many victories by Sylvester's trainees from the backstretch, which also involved watching pre-race preparation by Sylvester and the grooms as well as post-race procedures of cooling out and physical inspection. Sylvester, his wife Catherine, and their son John, lived in Garden City, New York, and followed the racing circuit of New York summers and Florida winters. John would go on to train the great Alydar and champion fillies Davona Dale, Before Dawn and Our Mims for Calumet Farm, as well as turf champion Sunshine Forever for Darby Dan Farm. The 24-day Saratoga racing season of that era gave us all a brief opportunity to catch up on family matters.

The backstretch of Saratoga Race Course is a special place, infused with the smell of liniment, and changing light patterns as summer evolves in ancient barns which have been home to so many racing immortals. I was a racing fan from the start, and I was impressed that the famous horses, owners, and trainers that I read about in the sports pages of major newspapers were right here in Saratoga Springs. Through my father and great-uncle, I got to meet some of them, which only added to the appeal of the backstretch.

I came back to all this in a professional way when Eric Wolferman and Mike Coleman hired me to work for the *Saratogian* in 1979 as a racing correspondent. There is nothing I enjoy more than going to the barns each morning for trainer interviews. The trainers are the directors of a daily ritual that has a rhythm you can feel during the racing season. As it proceeds I make time for just watching, perhaps at Clare Court, at the southern end of the track property, or in a lonely grandstand seat on a morning during the final days of the meeting.

It is at those moments when the historical weight of Saratoga Race Course hits me. This is the place of Ruthless, Hindoo, Man o'War, Ruffian and Secretariat. It is where men like William R. Travers, John Hunter, Leonard Jerome, August Belmont, Milton Sanford, William C. Whitney and others invested in thoroughbred racing. That it got started in 1863, in the middle of the Civil War, is in itself remarkable when one considers the negative impact of the war on racing centers of the South.

My interest in those early years of Saratoga Race Course led to this book. From the beginning, Saratoga attracted the best in racing. In our time, we are accustomed to descriptions of Saratoga as having racing of the highest class. It was no different in the 1860's; Saratoga Race Course was a premier summer meet from the start.

The 1870's and 1880's were a time of major expansion in the length of the racing season, and with it came some of the same issues we face today. Is there too much racing? Are there enough good horses? Is there dangerous competition from other tracks? How does all this fit with the people of Saratoga Springs? A continuing theme is that of ownership. Saratoga racing history is defined largely by people who do not live in the community. During the 1890's, Saratoga endured a time of poor management which bottomed out in 1896, a summer of no racing. The track, the industry, and the community are, more than one hundred years later, benefiting from the vision of William C. Whitney, who purchased the track in 1900.

I have enjoyed this study, and I hope it adds to your knowledge of thoroughbred racing in Saratoga Springs, as it has added to mine.

Michael Veitch
2004

Chapter I

FOUNDATIONS 1863-1869

In our time, the Triple Crown and Breeders' Cup represent the finest in American thoroughbred racing. Leading owners and trainers organize their schedules around them, hoping for the glory and long-term recognition that comes from victory in these famous races.

The Triple Crown consists of three famous races. They are the Kentucky Derby, Preakness Stakes, and Belmont Stakes. The Kentucky Derby, first run in 1875, is contested at Churchill Downs in Louisville, Kentucky. The Preakness Stakes, first run in 1873, is contested at Pimlico Race Course in Baltimore, Maryland. The Belmont Stakes, first run in 1867, is contested at Belmont Park in Elmont, New York. The Triple Crown is for three-year-old horses only. The Kentucky Derby opens the series on the first Saturday in May, followed by the Preakness Stakes two weeks later. The Belmont concludes the series, three weeks after the Preakness Stakes. The three races are run on a dirt surface.

The Breeders' Cup is an annual event for horses of all ages, and consists of several rich races contested on a single day. The races are run on both dirt and grass surfaces. The Breeders' Cup was first held in 1984, and has no fixed location. The Breeders' Cup is considered to be a year-end championship event, and is held at major tracks in North America.

Nearly equal in importance to the Triple Crown and Breeders' Cup are events such as the Kentucky Oaks, Florida Derby, Travers Stakes, Coaching Club American Oaks, Santa Anita Handicap, Turf Classic, Arlington Million and Metropolitan Handicap. When their day arrives, they are the center of attention of the vast sport-industry built around the thoroughbred. Sometimes, the thoroughbred is named Man o'War, Secretariat, or Ruffian. When that happens, the attention transcends racing and becomes part of the general public awareness of sports.

If there is a race track that has a place in the mind of the sports public, it is Saratoga Race Course, America's oldest extant thoroughbred facility. From the start, racing at Saratoga has held a lofty position. It rooted deeply and quickly in the heart of the Civil War, which raged from 1861 to 1865. Today, Saratoga racing is noted for its national quality, with champions like Point Given, Go for Wand, Holy Bull, Silverbulletday and Thunder Gulch winning major events. Nearly a century and a half ago, the same high standard existed at Saratoga.

Organized thoroughbred race meetings in Saratoga Springs began on August 3, 1863, at the Saratoga Trotting Course, a track of slightly more than seven furlongs which came to be known as Horse Haven. The trotting course had been built in conjunction with the New York State Fair, held in Saratoga Springs in 1847, and was the site of trotting and flat racing that year.[1] On September 16, 1847, the first recorded flat race at the trotting course was won by Lady Digby, won in straight heats over two opponents in 1:58 and 1:53 for the distance.

Saratoga Springs before the Civil War had a substantial tourist clientele, many of whom were supportive of racing. The State Fair attracted some 30,000 visitors, including former presidents Martin Van Buren and John Tyler. Saratoga's reputation as a fine place for horses was already national. Richard Ten Broeck shipped his great horse Lexington to Saratoga from New Orleans in 1854. A member of the National Museum of Racing's Hall of Fame, Lexington was the dominant runner of his day, winning six of seven starts before going on to a great stud career as the sire of top horses such as Norfolk, Asteroid, Tom Bowling, Kentucky, and Harry Bassett. Ten Broeck, hearing from the trotting community about the benefits of Saratoga Springs, sent Lexington to the Spa to await the completion of the Fashion Course on Long Island. Trotting events of national significance continued to be held in Saratoga Springs prior to 1863. The course also hosted flat races on September 17 and September 18, 1858, including hurdle races.

Before the Civil War, thoroughbred racing flourished in the South at courses in Alabama, Louisiana, Virginia, Mississippi, Tennessee, and South Carolina. The war disrupted the sport there, and control gradually passed to the North. A revival took place in the North, especially in New York and New Jersey, where the structure of the sport changed somewhat.[2] In the South, stamina was the key for champions, in four-mile events patterned on English racing. In contrast, the North featured two-mile races as well as races for two-year-olds at distances of one mile or less.

When the proprietors of Long Island race courses scheduled a summer break in 1863, the sport moved to Saratoga Springs for a four-day meeting at the trotting course. The meeting, organized and supported financially by John Morrissey, received extensive advance publicity. Horses from Canada, New Jersey, and Pennsylvania headed to Saratoga Springs for an event described as one of the greatest in years at the Spa.[3]

The meeting attracted thousands more spectators than the

trotting course could accommodate. Lizzie W., a filly, defeated the favored colt Captain Moore in the last two of three one-mile heats, timed in 1:50½ and 1:48½ in the opening event on August 3. In all, 26 horses ran at the first meeting, in a total of eight races over the four days. Lizzie W. was also a winner on closing day, August 6, at 1¼ miles. The second race on opening day, a two-mile event, was won by Sympathy, with Morrissey's horse J.B. Davidson finishing second.

The inaugural meeting was a big success. Morrissey, a prize fighter, gambler and politician, realized a better facility was necessary for subsequent meetings. The trotting course was not suited for thoroughbreds, since it was designed with long straight sections and tight turns, and measured only 66 feet wide.[4] In addition, because the course was lined by maple and pine trees, spectators were not able to see much of the contests.

Morrissey joined with three other men to purchase 125 acres of land across Union Avenue at $100 per acre, which today is Saratoga Race Course. They were William R. Travers, a leading New York City businessman; John R. Hunter, a Westchester sportsman; and Leonard Jerome, founder of Jerome Park Race Course and grandfather of British statesman Sir Winston Churchill.

The Travers Stakes, first run in 1864 at the new course, is named for Travers. Hunter became the first chairman of The Jockey Club, founded in 1894, while Jerome was considered a leading promoter of thoroughbred racing in the East.[5]

The new course was one mile in circumference, built upon a clay base of two inches with a sandy loam cushion.[6] The Saratoga Racing Association (SRA), with Travers as president, attracted horses from all sections of the United States, plus Canada, for the second race meeting in Saratoga Springs. In addition to Travers, officers of the SRA were vice-president Jerome, treasurer John H. White, and secretary Charles Wheatly. The executive committee of the SRA consisted of Hunter, owner of inaugural Travers Stakes winner Kentucky, plus George Osgood, James Marvin, Commodore Cornelius Vanderbilt, Erastus Corning, and John M.B. Davidson.

The accommodations at the new course, including a new covered grandstand with refreshment rooms, proved very popular with the sporting public and drew favorable reviews in the press. The *New York Times* reported a paid attendance of 6,345 for closing day, Saturday, August 6, 1864. As for the Travers Stakes, it has a special and prestigious place in the hearts of racing people. The Travers has been a race of champions for most of its history, during which it has often been as important as Triple Crown events.

The Travers Stakes was the first race of the 1864 meeting. It is the oldest stakes race in the United States for three-year-olds. The nation's oldest stakes race is the Phoenix Breeders' Cup at Keeneland, first run in 1831 as the Phoenix Hotel Stakes. The Queen's Plate, at Woodbine Race Track in Toronto, is also older than the Travers. It was first run in 1860 at Carleton Race Course, near Toronto.

The second meeting was another success, prompting the SRA to make further improvements to the new course for the 1865 meeting. The grandstand was enlarged and more train service was added on runs from Albany and Troy to Saratoga Springs. On March 21, 1865, the association was incorporated under New York law as the Saratoga Association for the Improvement of the Breed. The SRA was to hold its meetings on the grounds of Saratoga Race Course.

The Saratoga Cup was inaugurated at the 1865 meeting on the second day, August 8, and drew a crowd reported as more than 10,000. During just its third year, racing in Saratoga Springs was being compared to Goodwood and Royal Ascot, two famous courses in England. The six-day meeting of 1865 awarded $15,000 in purses and attracted many of the nation's leading sportsmen.

The Saratoga races were also big business with hotel proprietors, whose relationship with the racing community was at times uneasy. There was friction during the 1866 season when an anticipated extra day of racing, to be supported by the proprietors with $1,000 in purse money, failed to take place. Some proprietors had been demanding admission badges to the track, while the SRA had been hoping for their support for the extra day. The association was so upset with the situation that it threatened to move the races to another location, and reportedly had been offered $5,000 to do so.[7] Regardless of the bad feeling, thoroughbred racing continued to grow in stature at the fifth meeting in 1867. Two weeks before opening day, August 7, the association reported it would offer $11,000 to $12,000 in purses for the six-day meeting. Over 8,000 customers attended a beautiful opening day, witnessing the great filly Ruthless capture the fourth edition of the Travers Stakes.

Owned by Francis Morris, she was the most famous of his "Barbarous Battalion." The oldest was Ruthless, born in 1864, while Relentless was born in 1865 and Remorseless in 1867. They were three full sisters, each by the sire Eclipse out of the mare Barbarity. Relentless won the Saratoga Stakes in 1867 over General Duke, who captured the Belmont Stakes in 1868. Remorseless was considered the champion two-year-

Ruthless – owned by Francis Morris, the daughter of Eclipse won the inaugural Belmont Stakes and the fourth edition of the Travers Stakes in 1867.

old filly of 1869 by many experts, due to her victories in the Flash, Saratoga, Nursery and Annual stakes. Barbarity was also the mother of Regardless, another top filly owned by Morris. Born in 1871, she won the Flash Stakes in 1873 and Alabama Stakes in 1874 at Saratoga. Still another from this wonderful mare was the winning filly Merciless.

Ruthless began her racing career at Saratoga by finishing second to Red Wing in the Saratoga Stakes as a two-year-old of 1866. It was her first of 11 career starts, all of which were in races not restricted to fillies. After breaking her maiden two days later at Saratoga, on July 28, Ruthless did not race again until the fall Jerome Park meeting. She won the Nursery Stakes on October 1 at Jerome Park, and completed her season on October 10 in the Trial Stakes at Paterson, New Jersey, finishing second to stablemate Monday.

Ruthless opened her three-year-old season at Jerome Park on May 23, 1867, winning the Spring Stakes at six furlongs. The very next day, she won a purse event at 1¼ miles. Ruthless then finished second to Monday in the 1½-mile Jersey Derby at Paterson on June 4. She won the inaugural Belmont Stakes on June 19 at Belmont Park, defeating three colts at 15/8 miles. She did not race again until her victory in the Travers Stakes on August 7 at 1¾ miles. Five days later, Ruthless won the Sequel Stakes at Saratoga on August 12, at the distance of two miles. In her final career start, Ruthless finished second in the Jersey St. Leger, raced over 2¼ miles at Paterson on October 1. A training injury later that fall ended her career, during which she won seven of 11 starts, earning $11,000.

The Morris fillies were examples of the high class of Saratoga racing at this time. August Belmont, Leonard Jerome, Milton Sanford, and Col. David McDaniel were among the owners stabled at the Spa, for which the SRA built additional stalls for the six-day meeting of 1868. Belmont, a leading American banker, was the founder of the Belmont Stakes at Jerome Park in 1867. McDaniel owned the top horse Harry Bassett, the champion three-year-old of 1871. Another leading owner at the Spa was Maryland Governor Oden Bowie, who that summer was promoting his state's support of a proposed new race track.

Sanford, who had won the prestigious Saratoga Cup a few days earlier with Lancaster, hosted a dinner party on August 9 at which Gov. Bowie and several leading horsemen discussed the new track.[8] On that evening, Gov. Bowie reported that the State of Maryland and City of Baltimore were each contributing $25,000 toward the construction of the new track, on the grounds of today's Pimlico Race Course.[9]

To commemorate the opening of the new track, which was scheduled for the autumn of 1870, the group set up a race known as the Dinner Party Stakes, for three-year-olds at two miles. Pimlico opened on schedule and is the second oldest track in the nation behind Saratoga Race Course. Sanford won the Dinner Party Stakes with Preakness, the first stakes winner in Pimlico history. Preakness would later deadheat with Springbok in the Saratoga Cup of 1875, giving Sanford a second victory in the event.

Gov. Bowie, whose term of office ended in 1872, proclaimed a new race for the spring of 1873 to honor Sanford's horse. Known as the Preakness Stakes, the race became the middle jewel of the Triple Crown. Social affairs have always gone hand-in-hand with racing in Saratoga Springs. Seldom has one of those affairs had such a lasting effect on the sport as Sanford's on that long-ago summer evening!

The popularity of the sport with Saratoga tourists, and the respect held by American turfmen for the racing experience, caused the SRA to make more improvements for the seven-day meeting in 1869. Two new stables were built near the old trotting course and the main track was widened by 40 feet. Horsemen from New York, Louisiana, Tennessee, Missouri, Maryland, Illinois and New Jersey participated at the meeting. Saratoga officials, such as Gov. Bowie, Travers, and

Charles Wooley of the Buckeye Association, were comple-
mented by Morrissey's orderly supervision of the large crowds.
The officials, for example, ordered refunds to bettors who
backed Vauxhall in the Saratoga Cup of 1869, because they
considered rider John Ford's effort on the runner-up as questionable.

Private races, held on July 31, preceded the scheduled
opening day of August 4. Finesse, owned by Belmont, won in
a walkover as Hunter & Travers's Intrigue withdrew at $2,000
a side. Viley, Biddy Malone and Gen. Ewell were three competitors in a private sweepstakes consisting of two-mile heats
for four-year-olds at $1,000 each. Viley, owned by Bowie and
Hall, won in 3:42½ and 3:43. A third event, at $2,500 a side
for two-year-old fillies at 1 1/8 miles, was voided when one of
the competitors, Miss Alice, killed herself while running
through a fence on July 10.

In addition to the Travers Stakes, the customary opening-
day stakes race of the period, a new race called the Flash Stakes
was inaugurated in 1869. Drawing ten starters, it was won by
Remorseless, owned by Morris. Contemporary newspaper
accounts called the 1869 meeting the best ever at Saratoga.

CHAPTER II

EXPANSION AND CHALLENGE
1870-1890

The SRA expanded the 1870 season to 12 days, comprised of two sessions of six days each, one in July and one in August. The length of the Saratoga thoroughbred season now began a rapid expansion, reaching 40 days in 1882. An interesting aspect of the expanding racing season at the Spa was the earmarking of the profits of certain days for charity. The association also made many more improvements for the 1870 season. It built five more barns, bringing the total to 20, and put a new surface of loam on the main track. The old trotting course was shortened to six furlongs, due to the widening of Union Avenue, which today separates the former trotting course from the main track.

There was great anticipation in racing circles for the 1870 season. The *New York Times* reported that 120 horses were on the training grounds a full two weeks before the July 12 opening. Purses for the meeting were announced at $30,000, and again stables from the most important racing centers in the

United States came to Saratoga for the eighth Spa season. During the era of split meetings, the first one tended to have the greater concentration of top horses and stakes races.

One of the great thoroughbred events of the decade occurred at Saratoga Race Course on July 14, 1871. Although ten entered the seventh edition of the Saratoga Cup at 2¼ miles, the presence of Kentucky horseman John Harper's Longfellow and August Belmont's Kingfisher had the effect of reducing the field to a match between the two four-year-olds, the latter of which had won the Travers Stakes in 1870.

Before coming to Saratoga, Longfellow earned a reputation as America's best and most popular horse. Prior to the Saratoga Cup, he won the Monmouth Cup easily over Helmbold, the champion handicapper of 1870. In the Saratoga Cup, Longfellow was a three-length winner in 4:02¼. Each time Kingfisher tried him, Longfellow drew off. After the race, Belmont said he would bet Longfellow against any horse in the world.[1] Longfellow stayed in Saratoga for the entire meeting in 1871 and on August 19 he had a walkover at 2¾ miles. He then suffered a stunning upset by Helmbold on closing day, August 23, in a four-mile event contested on a sloppy track he didn't like.

Longfellow returned for the Saratoga Cup of 1872, which

created as much interest as the previous year's edition. Unbeaten in four starts prior to the Saratoga Cup, Longfellow faced John Morrissey's Defender and Col. David McDaniel's Harry Bassett, winner of the Travers Stakes in 1871. Early in the race, perhaps after a half-mile, Longfellow twisted the shoe on his left front foot and it spiked upward into his foot. Despite this awful injury, Longfellow pressed Harry Bassett the entire way, losing by only a length while forcing an American record of 3:59 for 2¼ miles. Police had to restrain the crowd during the stretch run, which was throwing hats and canes into the air as it cheered the courageous Longfellow in what turned out to be his final race. The Hall of Fame horse retired with 13 wins and two seconds from 16 starts, earning $11,200.

The year 1872 was also memorable for the inauguration of Saratoga's great filly race, the Alabama Stakes. The Alabama came by its name courtesy of William Cottrill, a Mobile native who was a leading thoroughbred owner at Fair Grounds Race Track in New Orleans, Louisiana, in the 1870's and 1880's. Cottrill also raced at Saratoga, where he was offered a race named in his honor. Cottrill, who had served in the Army of the Confederate States of America, suggested the race would be better served if named for his state.[2] He was one of several southern sportsmen whose support was an important aspect of Saratoga racing during its first few decades.

Four fillies lined up for the inaugural Alabama Stakes. They were Belmont's favored Woodbine; David D. Withers's Mimi; Clay, Strongfield and Glean's Nema; and Col. David McDaniel's Sue Rider. Mimi took the lead at the start, followed by Woodbine, Nema and Sue Rider. The group remained in that order until the half-mile pole, when Woodbine gained the lead and gradually widened her margin on the way to victory. Nema was second, Sue Rider third, and Mimi fourth. Mimi crossed the finish line second, but was disqualified to fourth for crossing over Woodbine in the stretch. Woodbine completed 1 1/8 miles in 2:06¼ and Belmont received $2,650 as the winner's purse.

Winning the first Alabama Stakes was in line with the contribution to New York racing by August Belmont and his family. The Belmont Stakes, third leg of the American Triple Crown, is named for Belmont. His son, August Belmont II, won the Belmont Stakes in 1916 with Friar Rock and in 1917 with Hourless. August Belmont IV won the Belmont Stakes with Caveat in 1983.

Another prominent family to lend early support to Saratoga racing was that of Stephen Sanford, the builder of Hurricana Stud in Amsterdam, New York. He began racing at

24

Saratoga Race Course in the 1870's. The names of his horses reflected his love of the Mohawk River Valley and its history, especially as it pertained to the Indians who comprised the Iroquois Confederacy. Noted runners carrying Sanford's purple and gold silks included Caughnawaga, Chuctanunda, Molly Brant, Mohawk II, Sir John Johnson, and Herkimer.

Sanford's custom was to train his horses at Hurricana Stud and point them for the Saratoga meeting. In the late nineteenth and early twentieth centuries, Sanford won the Hopeful Stakes, Saratoga Cup, Saratoga Special, and Alabama Stakes. The Sanford Memorial Stakes, inaugurated at Saratoga Race Course in 1913, is named in his honor. His descendants today carry on a tradition that has all but vanished in American racing; they pay for and award the sterling silver cup given to the winner of the Sanford Memorial Stakes. The event gained a lasting place in racing history when the immortal Man o' War finished second to Upset in the 1919 edition. It was the only time Man o' War lost in 21 career starts.

John Morrissey introduced the new feature of pari-mutuel betting at the 1872 meeting, based upon the French system of "Paris mutuels." Working with a three percent takeout, Morrissey returned the pools on a pro-rated basis to the winning bettors, who wagered $5 per ticket. For example, on the steeplechase race for July 15, 360 tickets were sold, for a gross of $1,800. Removing the $54 takeout left $1,746 in the pool. The 59 winning tickets divided up $1,746, which rounded out to a return of $30 each. However, the betting aspect of racing at Saratoga was removed to the far eastern end of the grounds, to keep it separate from racing fans who attended for sporting reasons only.

It was at this time the SRA began the practice of adding "extra" days to the Saratoga meeting with proceeds going to local organizations. In 1874, Saratoga Springs public schools and the Saratoga Rowing Association each benefited from an extra day.

The year 1874 was another strong one for Saratoga racing, marked by noteworthy performances in the final week of the season, long after the most important stakes races had been run. Aristides won a juvenile handicap by ten lengths at one mile. The next year he won the inaugural Kentucky Derby and finished third to D'Artagnan in the 12th edition of the Travers Stakes. Also in the final week, Fellowcraft erased Lexington's record of 7:19¾ for four miles, set in 1855. Fellowcraft was timed in 7:19½, carrying 108 pounds as a four-year-old. Lexington set his record as a five-year-old under 103 pounds.

The SRA lengthened the Saratoga Race Course meeting to 21 days in 1877, seven more days than in 1876. A main reason for the increase was to induce horsemen to stay at Saratoga and not go to Monmouth Park Race Track in New Jersey, which had opened in 1870. The existence of Monmouth Park put pressure on the eastern horse population. The situation was compounded by a horse sickness that hampered most of the 1876 meeting at Saratoga.

The SRA was concerned about a second straight difficult meeting, and Morrissey let his nerves loose. He wrote a letter to the *New York Times* dated July 10, 1877, in which he threatened SRA weight penalties to horses which raced elsewhere after June 25. His letter also promised 30 additional races at Saratoga exclusively for horses which did not race after June 25.

Added to the pressures of conflicting dates and available horses for entries was another problem facing the SRA. The August Belmont horses were ill and would be on the sidelines for the 1877 season. Still, the meeting became a success, marked by both good attendance and weather. Leading owners supported Morrissey and the association despite the weight penalties, which some accepted and still participated at Saratoga. Subscriptions for the stakes events of 1878 and 1879 were strong, indicating continued support.

Duke of Magenta – owned by George L. Lorillard, the son of Lexington won four stakes at Saratoga in 1878, including the Travers Stakes. He also won the Preakness Stakes that year.

Morrissey, however, would not live to see the 1878 Saratoga meeting. He died in Saratoga Springs at the Adelphi Hotel on May 1, 1878, at age 47. Along with Albert Spencer and Charles Reed, he owned one-third of the stock in the SRA.

The 27-day meeting of 1878 was lucrative for the SRA and profitable for horsemen. Purses were a record $74,605 and contemporary accounts reported large crowds throughout the season, which saw 153 horses compete in 108 races.

The star of the 1878 season was George L. Lorillard's Duke of Magenta, who arrived at the Spa while creating one of the great three-year-old campaigns in American racing history. Trained by R. Wyndham Walden, Duke of Magenta won the Preakness Stakes in his seasonal debut. Duke of Magenta kicked off a string of five straight Preakness scores for Walden, who won seven editions of the race. Duke of Magenta also won the Withers Stakes and Belmont Stakes before coming to Saratoga.

Duke of Magenta won the Travers Stakes on July 20, the Sequel Stakes on August 2, the Kenner Stakes on August 13, and the Harding Stakes on August 20. He would go on to win 11 stakes races from 12 starts as a three-year-old in 1878.

In 1879, Saratoga Springs hotels sponsored races at the meeting. They were the Grand Union, Clarendon, Windsor, and Congress Hall, with the proprietors putting up from $500 to $1,000 in money added to the subscription fees. And the SRA at this time was emboldened to guarantee a minimum of 100 races per Saratoga season. New owners such as James R. Keene, the Wall Street magnate, and E. J. "Lucky" Baldwin, of California, were represented at Saratoga in 1879. Later on, Keene raced greats such as Domino, Commando, Colin and Sysonby, while Baldwin's Santa Anita Stable won clusters of Saratoga stakes races in the 1880's with stars such as Los Angeles, the champion two-year-old filly of 1887. The 1879 season was also marked by the "clanging of the bell," which alerted jockeys to weigh out prior to the race.[3]

Purses reached $94,025 in 1880, reflecting the continually increasing length of the season, which now stood at 34 days. The association put up more than $57,000, with hotel proprietors, steamship lines, and subscription fees accounting for the rest. Two Hall of Fame greats, Hindoo and Luke Blackburn, performed at Saratoga during an outstanding summer of racing. *Krik's Guide to the Turf*, in its 1880 edition, lauded Saratoga Race Course for its fast track, steeplechase course of 2¾ miles with 36 jumps including two over water, and its refreshing environment for thoroughbreds.[4]

Hindoo arrived as an unbeaten juvenile in seven starts.

He would complete his two-year-old season with two shocking losses at Saratoga in the Windsor Hotel Stakes and Day Boat Line Stakes. Purchased by the Dwyer Bros. from Daniel Swigert for $15,000 at the end of his juvenile season, Hindoo returned to Saratoga in 1881 to win the Travers, Sequel, United States Hotel, and Kenner stakes. According to the *Spirit of the Times*, "The contest for the Travers was Hindoo's crowning effort, and in all respects, was the greatest race of his life."[5]

Hindoo won 18 straight races that year, including the Kentucky Derby, Tidal Stakes, Monmouth Sweepstakes, and New Jersey St. Leger. He retired as a four-year-old with a record of 30-3-2 from 35 starts and earnings of $71,875.

The Dwyers also owned Luke Blackburn, who won 22 of 24 starts as a three-year-old of 1880. At Saratoga, he won the Summer Handicap, United States Hotel Stakes, Grand Union Prize, and Kenner Stakes, the last of which was the richest race at the 1880 meeting. Luke Blackburn was brought back to the races as a four-year-old, but was retired after breaking down in his second start. He earned $49,460 in his career, with a record of 25-6-2 in 39 starts.

The SRA added three days to its meeting of 1881, bringing the total to 37. Several new stakes races were inaugurated, foremost among them the Spinaway, the nation's oldest stakes race for two-year-old fillies. Sparked by the victory of Iroquois in the Epsom Derby, there was tremendous interest in racing that year. Iroquois was the first American-bred horse to win the Epsom Derby, a race begun in 1780. The Saratoga season of 1881 was dominated by the stables of the Dwyer Bros., Belmont, Jerome, the Lorillards, and Charles Reed.

With Hindoo a seeming reflection of the SRA's confidence in Saratoga racing at this time, the association announced a meeting of 40 days for 1882. It was another very good season, with the great Miss Woodford winning the Spinaway and the remarkable Thora adding to her impressive Saratoga record.

In addition to the Spinaway, Miss Woodford, owned by George Bowen, Catesby Woodford, Ezekiel F. Clay, and the Dwyer Bros., won the Misses Stakes at Saratoga in 1882, the Alabama Stakes the following season, and the First Sweepstakes in 1886. Her career included a streak of 16 straight victories over three seasons at ages three, four and five. When she retired at the end of her six-year-old season, she had earned $118,270 with a record of 37-7-2 in 48 starts. Miss Woodford was the first horse bred and raised in America to earn more than $100,000.

As a two-year-old filly of 1880, Thora, owned by Charles Reed, began an amazing collection of Saratoga victories by upsetting Hindoo in the Day Boat Line Stakes. In 1881, Thora won the Alabama Stakes, the Clarendon Hotel Stakes, and Baden-Baden Handicap. As a four-year-old in 1882, Thora won the Excelsior Sweepstakes and the Saratoga Cup, the latter described by the *New York Times* as won by 60 yards while "pulled double," meaning Thora's rider held her tightly and did not have to urge her during the race.[6]

These were good times for Saratoga Race Course and its host community. More stables were being built, including private ones owned by George and Pierre Lorillard and August Belmont. The racing seasons of 1881 and 1882 were the longest ever, and the great hotels of the village were enjoying prosperity.

At this juncture, though, there were warning signs that thoroughbred racing at the springs was headed for difficulty. Purses at Monmouth Park were as good as those of Saratoga, luring away top horses for its stakes races. The Belmont and Lorillard stables also raced at Monmouth, and on several days of head-to-head competition with Saratoga, the New Jersey track offered better purses. There was also debate about the long racing season and that segment of the Saratoga summer scene. Henry Clair, proprietor of the Grand Union Hotel, was among a group of large hotel proprietors who were unhappy with six weeks of racing over a two-month period, finding racing activity and its gamblers not necessarily in Saratoga's best interest. Clair, and others like him, preferred conventions and hotel-related activities for their businesses, while smaller proprietors found the racing clientele to be very profitable.[7]

For the 1883 season, the SRA reduced the Saratoga racing season to 35 days. As the decade proceeded, the number of days at the meeting declined from the high of 40 in 1882 to 30 in 1889. The trend of reduction was a result of increasing competition from Monmouth Park and Brighton Beach, on Long Island. Their proximity to metropolitan New York produced profitable gate revenue. In addition, the gambling aspect of racing continued to trouble some Saratogians, who were hearing reports of race results that suggested foul play.

Despite these problems, there were bright spots as the decade of the 1880's played out. During the middle to late years of the decade, E. J. Baldwin's stable compiled an enviable record at Saratoga. Included among his winners were Volante, winner of the Flash, Beverwyck, Excelsior and Sequel; Mission Belle, winner of the Spinaway and Misses; Grisette, winner of the Spinaway and Alabama; and Los Angeles, winner of the Spinaway, Equity, Foxhall, Pocahantas, Kenner, Excelsior and Congress Hall.

Baldwin's best may have been Emperor of Norfolk, purchased as a yearling for $2,550 in 1886.[8] As a two-year-old at Saratoga, he won the Saratoga Stakes on August 4, the Virginia Stakes on August 9, the Kentucky Stakes on August 11, and the Tennessee Stakes on August 19. His juvenile season also included races in Illinois, New Jersey, Washington, D. C., and Missouri. Emperor of Norfolk won 12 of 18 races, earning $36,490. At age three, the California-bred Emperor of Norfolk won the rich American Derby at 1½ miles, as well as the Swift, Brooklyn Derby, and Sheridan stakes. His career ended after his victory in the Sheridan on July 4. Emperor of Norfolk, elected to the Hall of Fame in 1988, won 21 of 29 starts, earning $72,400. He was considered a champion in each campaign, as well as the top horse in training as a three-year-old in 1888.

Emperor of Norfolk did not make it to Saratoga in 1888, a year during which Baldwin's Los Angeles was in the midst of her great work at the Spa. In 1887 she won the Spinaway Stakes and Equity Stakes, while in 1888 Los Angeles won the Foxhall Stakes at 1 5/8 miles, the Kenner Stakes at two miles while conceding weight to her male opponents, and the Pocahantas Stakes at a mile and 500 yards.

The Kenner Stakes was a prestigious event in its heyday,

having been won by Harry Bassett (1871), Duke of Magenta (1878), Luke Blackburn (1880) and Hindoo (1881). The Kenner was named for Duncan F. Kenner, a president of the Louisiana Jockey Club and leading owner at thoroughbred tracks in that state.

At Saratoga in 1889, Los Angeles won the Excelsior Stakes at 1¼ miles and the Congress Hall Stakes in straight heats at six furlongs. She won the one-mile California Stakes in 1890 on July 26, followed by a repeat score in the Excelsior Stakes three days later at 1¼ miles. Los Angeles then won the Kearney Stakes at 1½ miles on August 5 and the Merchants Stakes at 1 5/8 miles on August 7.

The Baldwin mare was not yet done at Saratoga Race Course. In 1890, she captured the Beverwyck Stakes at a mile and 500 yards on August 19 and the Congress Hall Stakes in six-furlong heats on August 23. Los Angeles carried on as a six-year-old in 1891, winning the Congress Hall on August 7. She then won the Morrissey Stakes at 1 5/8 miles on August 22 in a walkover, followed by a victory in the historic Saratoga Cup five days later at two miles.

Over 600 horses were stabled on the SRA grounds for the 1889 meeting of 30 days, with five races per day as the schedule. But the continuing and growing controversy over gambling, and the sale of the track to Gottfried Walbaum of

New Jersey, would usher in a difficult decade for Saratoga thoroughbred racing.

Many Saratogians, as well as longtime seasonal tourists, were not happy with the gambling atmosphere that surrounded the track and various betting parlors in the village. They longed for a return to the summer seasons of professional conventions, artistic gatherings, and hotel-centered activities that were so popular in pre-racing days. The hotels continued their programs in the last decades of the nineteenth century, but often forbade their employees from going to the track. They were in agreement with local newspaper publisher Spencer Trask, who was finding many allies as he mounted an anti-gambling crusade.

The competition from Monmouth Park and other tracks kept chipping away at the Saratoga meeting. One of the track's major owners, Charles Reed, who campaigned Thora, became discouraged and sold his interest in 1887 to Albert Spencer, who would hold on for four more years until selling his interest. There were also reports of fixed races at Saratoga, causing some owners to prefer racing elsewhere. A pattern was developing at this time in Saratoga racing: owners would keep their stakes engagements at Saratoga Race Course, and little else. Another trend utilized Saratoga as merely a place of respite for horses, between the spring and fall meets in the New York City area.

Walbaum, an avid gambler, was at this time a part owner of the Guttenberg Race Track in New Jersey. Unlike patrons such as August Belmont, John Hunter, Leonard Jerome and others interested in sport and breed improvement, Walbaum equated track ownership with gambling profit.

CHAPTER III

DECLINE AND RECOVERY
1891-1900

Gottfried Walbaum was winning races, as a horse owner, at the Saratoga Race Course meeting in 1890. According to his memoirs (transcribed by Frank Tannehill Jr. during 1930-1931), he purchased Saratoga Race Course from Albert Spencer in November 1891.[1] Walbaum owned 75 percent of the track stock, with partners accounting for the other 25 percent. The price, according to Walbaum, was $250,000, although at least one other account places the figure at $375,000.[2]

Walbaum constructed a new 5,000-seat grandstand in time for the 1892 meeting, which ran for 30 days from July 25 to September 3. In his memoirs, Walbaum claimed to originate the post parade at the 1892 meeting, bringing the horses out to the track ten to 20 minutes early so the fans could see them. In 1893, he paraded all the horses stabled at Horse Haven to the track before the first race on August 10, in conjunction with the association's first annual garden party.[3]

Despite his innovations, the quality of Saratoga racing entered a period of decline under Walbaum's ownership, especially when compared to Monmouth Park and the tracks in metropolitan New York. In 1893, Saratoga purses for the 30-day meeting were only $137,050, while Monmouth Park awarded $357,600 over 46 days; Coney Island awarded $242,600 over 26 days; the New York Jockey Club awarded $239,700 over 29 days; and Brooklyn awarded $226,450 over 30 days. In terms of daily average purses among these five tracks, Saratoga ranked last at $4,568. Coney Island was first at $9,330, followed by the New York Jockey Club at $8,265, Monmouth Park at $7,773 and Brooklyn at $7,548.[4]

In 1893, Walbaum changed the post time to 11:30 a.m., three hours earlier than the traditional 2:30 p.m. In doing so, he added lunch, entertainment, program printing, and even barbers at the track. This move alienated downtown merchants and others on the Saratoga scene who were accustomed to planning their days around afternoon racing.

The 1894 season started with high hopes, with many top owners and horses at Saratoga. It would not end that way. On opening day, July 23, Pierre Lorillard won the Flash Stakes with Liza, while Byron McClelland won the Travers Stakes with Henry of Navarre. Phil Dwyer, Foxhall and James R.

Keene, "Lucky" Baldwin, Joseph E. Seagram, and William Hendrie were also racing at Saratoga in 1894.

Henry of Navarre's Travers Stakes victory came in the midst of a terrific campaign during which he made 20 starts in the best of company from May to October in 1894. At the beginning of the season he placed to older horses in the Brooklyn and Metropolitan handicaps. After a narrow loss to Domino in the Withers Stakes, Henry of Navarre won 14 of his next 16 starts, including the Belmont Stakes and Travers. Following his Travers score, he captured the Foxhall Stakes, an allowance, and the Iroquois Stakes at Saratoga. Henry of Navarre won 29 of 42 starts in his career, and was off the board only twice, earning $68,985. His other major victories included the Manhattan, Municipal and Suburban handicaps. Henry of Navarre was elected to the Hall of Fame in 1985.

On July 25, two days after Henry of Navarre's Travers victory, Walbaum won four of the six races on the card with horses he owned, and on which he wagered. The very next day, he was the center of a dispute with owner Harry Morris, whose horse Peacemaker won the United States Hotel Stakes. The winner's share was announced as $2,000, which was the association's guaranteed value. But Morris accused the association of withholding the United States Hotel's contribution of $1,000, as well as the entrance and starting fees worth $420. Morris threatened to go to the newly-formed Jockey Club with his complaint, and eventually received nearly $1,000 more.

Walbaum engendered further controversy at the 1894 meeting when he returned the post time to 2:30 p.m. one week into the season. Critics charged him with accommodating heavy bettors who wanted to sleep late after a night of gambling at the Club House Casino in Congress Park. Walbaum changed it again to 1 p.m. and left it there for the remainder of the season.

His track management, his reputed involvement in several bookmaking operations, his victories in races of questionable integrity, and his disregard for Saratoga citizens combined to undermine thoroughbred racing in the village. Several owners withdrew their horses from stakes engagements because of the post time changes. With more than two weeks remaining of the 1894 schedule, many owners left Saratoga for Jerome Park and Sheepshead Bay, walking away from the remaining 12 stakes events at the Spa.

Citizen anger with Walbaum was growing, and in village circles there was talk of building a new track outside the tax district, while at the same time rezoning Saratoga Race Course to inside the district in an attempt to tax Walbaum out of existence.[5]

The Saratoga Racing Association announced a 40-day meeting for 1895, an ambitious schedule that fell 12 days short due to the unhappiness with Walbaum. New anti-gambling laws were also on the books, which kept the betting public away from the track. The *New York Times* listed attendance at a mere 400 for the card of Monday, August 5. The next day, the association announced it would close after 28 days of racing, on August 23, the day before Sheepshead Bay opened its fall meeting.

Another aspect of these rough times for Saratoga Race Course was the discontinuance of prestigious stakes races. The Travers Stakes, the oldest stakes race for three-year-olds in the United States, was not run in 1896, 1898, 1899 or 1900. The Alabama Stakes, one of America's most important events for three-year-old fillies, was not run in 1893, 1894, 1895, 1896, nor in 1898, 1899 or 1900. The Spinaway Stakes, the oldest in the United States for two-year-old fillies, was not run during 1892-1900.

There was no thoroughbred racing in Saratoga Springs in 1896. In an article for the *Saratogian*, Landon Manning, former sports editor for the newspaper and the author of two books on Saratoga racing, noted that Walbaum had been removed from the track presidency in 1895 due to his conviction in New Jersey on a felony assault charge. According to Manning, The Jockey Club, formed in 1894, was considered a possible purchaser of Saratoga Race Course. Walbaum, serving a prison term in 1895, was said to be considering the sale. But when he received an unexpected pardon from the New Jersey Court of Pardons, he decided to keep the track.[6]

Local events also played a part in the dismal circumstances of the 1895 season. Village authorities threatened to close every gambling venue in Saratoga Springs before the racing season began. Anti-gambling reformers, such as New York State Senator Edgar Truman Brackett, had for many years chafed at the gambling activities in the Club House Casino, now operated by Richard Canfield. Sen. Brackett was also angry about the bookmakers at the track and the gambling houses in the village.

One such house was owned by Caleb Mitchell, who for decades was an investor in Saratoga Springs and who at various times had served as an elected village official. Sen. Brackett, in 1892, introduced a bill – which became law – that enabled the village trustees of Saratoga Springs to elect the village president, rather than the public. Sen. Brackett's goal was to remove Mitchell from office, in accordance with the wishes of Saratogians who did not believe the village president should own a gambling house. The trustees indeed removed Mitchell, and replaced him with Charles S. Sturges of the Saratoga Telephone Company. In 1895, Sturges ordered the gambling houses closed and they complied, including Canfield's Club House.[7]

Gambling *was* permitted at the track in 1895, but in a manner which discouraged the regular heavy players who were Saratoga Race Course fixtures. According to Manning's piece for the *Saratogian*, no betting rings were allowed at the track and all wagers were made on credit until the end of the program. The big bettors left Saratoga that summer, causing a major loss of revenue for the association. At the close of the 1895 season, track management announced there would be no racing in 1896. However, Manning noted, The Jockey Club did leave open dates from July 1 to August 15 in case Walbaum changed his mind.

When racing returned to Saratoga Springs in 1897, the meeting of 22 days was the shortest since the 21-day session of 1877. The racing was highlighted by J. E. Madden's great young colt Hamburg winning the Flash Stakes under 129 pounds and the Congress Hall Stakes under 134 pounds. Hamburg was a tonic for Saratoga fans, adding to the excitement over the resumption of racing at the track.

Hamburg won 12 of 16 races as a two-year-old, finishing second three times and third on the other occasion. In his third and final appearance at Saratoga, he was upset by Archduke in the Grand Union Hotel Stakes, carrying 129 pounds to his rival's 117. Hamburg later went on to secure a championship as the best two-year-old male with a victory in the Great Eastern Handicap that fall under 135 pounds. He led all the way while conceding from 11 to 26 pounds to 13 opponents. The good runners Archduke and Bowling Brook were fifth and eighth, respectively.

Hamburg made his three-year-old debut in the Belmont Stakes of 1898, suffering a stunning upset to finish third behind Bowling Brook and Previous, a pair he had beaten on numerous occasions in 1897. Hamburg made four more starts and won them all, taking the Spring Special, Swift, Lawrence Realization, and Brighton Cup. The last two were at 1 5/8 miles and 2¼ miles, respectively, and in them he defeated the winners of the Futurity, Kentucky Derby, Brooklyn Handicap, and Withers. Hamburg retired after the Brighton Cup and was considered Horse of the Year. He posted a career record of 16-3-2 from 21 starts with earnings of $61,455.

The Brighton Cup was run at the Brighton Beach track, which was running concurrently with the first two weeks of the Saratoga meeting of 1898. Such competition, along with Walbaum's eroding reputation, turned the 1898 season into a major loser for the Saratoga Racing Association. There were only four stakes races during the 27-day meeting, as the Travers, Spinaway and Alabama were not run. Excluding the 1896 cancellation of racing, the Travers Stakes had been run without interruption from 1864 to 1897. As a result, several top New York owners, including August Belmont, remained on Long Island to await the fall Sheepshead Bay meeting.

Walbaum further angered the racing community by trying to force bettors to wager with his bookmakers. He also continued tinkering with the post times, moving them to later afternoon hours in order to accept the betting pools in western parts of the United States. This was in violation of rules of the state and The Jockey Club.

Rumors circulated routinely that Belmont, John Sanford, and others were interested in buying Saratoga Race Course, but Walbaum would not let go.[8] His last year as operator of the track was 1900, a year in which many leading Eastern horses came to Saratoga only as a freshening for the rich fall races at Sheepshead Bay. Their lack of participation on the Saratoga track was additional proof of the diminished stature of Saratoga thoroughbred racing under Walbaum's rule. The state Racing

WILLIAM C. WHITNEY
The great sportsman led a syndicate which purchased Saratoga Race Course in 1900, and undertook improvements which revitalized the track at the beginning of the 20th Century.

and Wagering Board balked at granting dates for 1901 to Walbaum when he insisted upon three or four weeks of exclusive racing with no competition from downstate tracks.[9]

Into this state of affairs stepped William C. Whitney, who announced on November 1, 1900, that he would shortly acquire Saratoga Race Course as the head of a syndicate which included several members of The Jockey Club. According to the *New York Times*, the Whitney syndicate acquired a majority of the stock on November 8, with the remaining shares going to local investors.[10]

A contemporary account in *Mansey's Magazine* placed Whitney's outlay at $250,000, and listed John Sanford, P. J. Dwyer, Perry Belmont, Alfred Featherstone, Thomas Hitchcock, F. R. Hitchcock, and R. R. Wilson as syndicate members.[11]

Whitney undertook a massive upgrading of the Saratoga Race Course facilities. He purchased the land that today is known as the Oklahoma Training Track, as well as the Horse Haven grounds. The main track was reconstructed and the grandstand repaired and improved. The Oklahoma, a one-mile track with a seven-furlong turf course, was opened in 1904. The cost of these projects was $500,000.[12] The main track reconstruction resulted in the oval of 1 1/8 miles of today, the former having been at one mile, plus a new steeple-chase course in the infield.[13]

All was right again with Saratoga thoroughbred racing. The 1901 season, thanks to The Jockey Club's interest in the betterment of the sport in New York, would have four weeks of top racing without major competition from downstate tracks. Large crowds were back at Saratoga, encouraged by the reputation of the Saratoga Racing Association president Whitney and his partners. Business was so good that by 1902, Whitney reported, the association was out of debt and would show a profit of $80,000 to $90,000.[14]

Whitney also restored the high-class stakes program at Saratoga. The Alabama, Spinaway and Travers all resumed in 1901, as did the fabled Saratoga Cup, which had not been run since 1891. Two new races for juveniles, the Adirondack for fillies and the Saratoga Special for colts, were inaugurated in 1901. Winners of the former include champions Busher (1944), Talking Picture (1973), and Smart Angle (1979), while greats such as Colin (1907), Regret (1914), Top Flight (1931), Whirlaway (1940), Native Dancer (1952), and Bold Forbes (1975) have won the Special. The Hopeful Stakes was inaugurated in 1903, and has produced winners such as Man o'War (1919), Nashua (1954), Buckpasser (1965), Secretariat (1972) and Affirmed (1977).

Also during the Whitney revival, private stables on the

grounds of Saratoga Race Course were being built by August Belmont, F. R. Hitchcock, John E. Madden, and the Sanford family.[15]

The Sanfords would open the new century with a run of victories in Saratoga's most important races. The Sanfords bred and raised their stock at Hurricana Stud in Amsterdam, about 25 miles west of Saratoga Springs. As mentioned previously, they trained their horses at Hurricana Stud in preparation for the Saratoga Race Course meeting. That meant that many of their horses didn't start until the summer meeting, yet they were able to compete with the powerful stables of Whitney, Belmont, and others who raced downstate on a season-long basis.

A few weeks before Saratoga opened, the Sanfords raced their horses in private trials at their training track in Amsterdam. One of the trials was public and known as the Sanford Matinee. It often drew 10,000 spectators, and Gen. Sanford would hire a band to add to the sporting atmosphere. The best Sanford runner may have been Mohawk II, winner of the Hopeful Stakes in 1905 under 130 pounds. Mohawk II was a son of Sanford's Rockton, winner of the Saratoga Cup in 1901. Mohawk II was also a half-brother to Sanford's Caughnawaga, winner of the Saratoga Handicap and Saratoga Cup in 1905.

Another classy Sanford runner was Molly Brant, winner of the Adirondack Stakes in 1902 and the Saranac Stakes in 1903. In 1904, she won the Merchants and Citizens Handicap and Delaware Handicap. In 1905 Molly Brant won the Delaware Handicap again, this time defeating Horse of the Year Beldame, and Roseben, both of which would gain entrance into the Hall of Fame. The Sanfords also campaigned Kenyetto, winner of the Alabama and Huron Stakes in 1907. In some polls, Kenyetto was champion three-year-old filly.

Saratoga thoroughbred racing would suffer another interruption in 1911 and 1912, when New York racing was shut down by the Directors' Criminal Liability Act of 1910, which held track owners responsible for any open betting. During this bleak time, Sanford raced his horses at Blue Bonnets Race Track in Montreal. Yet, during the two-year ban, some top New York stables still came to Whitney's Oklahoma Training Track to school their youngsters.[16] One group belonged to Saratoga Racing Association president Richard T. Wilson, while another belonged to the Beverwyck Stable of Saratogian Frank Nolan. The Nolan Stables today are part of the Fasig-Tipton horse auction property in Saratoga Springs.

It must have been a haunting scene, but one which nonetheless underlined the love of Saratoga by thoroughbred people.

Saratoga Race Course had seen its share of trouble, particularly the period of decline during the Walbaum era which hit bottom with the cancellation of the 1896 season. And it would close once again, in 1943, 1944 and 1945, due to World War II travel restrictions. However, the Saratoga races for those three seasons were conducted at Belmont Park.

Saratoga today commands the highest respect in the racing community. That is the legacy of the nineteenth century founders, whose accomplishments are reviewed in this book. William R. Travers, John Hunter, Leonard Jerome, John Morrissey and others did not just create any race track. They created and sustained a track that represented quality from the beginning. Hall of Fame horses such as Ruthless, Longfellow, Hindoo, Emperor of Norfolk, Luke Blackburn and Henry of Navarre raced at Saratoga in the nineteenth century.

William C. Whitney's revival made it possible for successive generations of racing fans to see champions such as Man o'War, Whirlaway, Tom Fool, Native Dancer,

Buckpasser, Secretariat, Affirmed, and Holy Bull continue the great tradition of Saratoga racing throughout the twentieth century and into the twenty-first.

NINETEENTH CENTURY RACING DATES AT SARATOGA RACE COURSE

YEAR	NO. OF DAYS	CALENDAR DATES
1863	4	August 3-6
1864	4	August 2-6
1865	6	August 7-12
1866	6	July 24-30
1867	6	August 7-13
1868	6	August 5-11
1869	7	July 31-August 10
1870	12	*July 14-20, August 12-18
1871	12	*July 12-18, August 16-23
1872	12	*July 13-19, August 17-23
1873	11	*July 24-August 1, August 5-16
1874	14	*July 25-August 4, August 8-22
1875	11	*July 24-August 4, August 10-21
1876	14	*July 25-August 3, August 8-23
1877	21	*July 21-August 9, August 11-30
1878	27	*July 20-August 8, August 10-29
1879	26	*July 19-August 2, August 5-20
1880	34	*July 17-31, August 5-28

1881	37	*July 16-August 3, August 4-27
1882	40	*July 11-August 1, August 2-26
1883	35	*July 21-August 10, August 11-30
1884	33	*July 19-August 8, August 9-28
1885	33	July 21-August 29
1886	30	July 24-August 28
1887	29	July 22-August 30
1888	30	July 24-August 30
1889	30	July 25-August 29
1890	30	July 24-August 28
1891	30	July 23-August 27
1892	30	July 25-September 3
1893	30	July 24-August 30
1894	30	July 23-August 25
1895	28	July 20-August 23
1896	0	NO RACING
1897	22	July 28-August 21
1898	27	July 28-August 27
1899	27	July 26-August 25
1900	22	August 1-25

NOTE: This list of racing dates is a compilation of various trade publications, books, and newspapers, all of which appear in the bibliography. During the years of two listings of calendar dates, beginning with 1870 and ending with 1884, the Saratoga Racing Association conducted two meetings.

Appendix B

TRIVIA

… Hurdle racing began at Saratoga Race Course during the 1864 season. A two-mile race was held on Saturday, August 6, with eight hurdles, spaced at four to each mile. Their height was six feet, three inches.

… Finishing fifth in the Saratoga Stakes of 1869 was a gelding named Kelso. In the mid-20th century another Kelso, also a gelding, was America's only five-time Horse of the Year, winning the honor during 1960-1964.

… Saratoga's most important race for two-year-olds, the Hopeful Stakes, was first run in 1903. Its winners include Regret, Native Dancer, Buckpasser, Secretariat, and Affirmed. There was a Hopeful Stakes for two-year-olds in the 1870's and 1880's at Monmouth Park, which had its inaugural meeting in 1870.

… Aristides won a race for two-year-olds at one mile in August

1874, at Saratoga Race Course. He won the inaugural Kentucky Derby in 1875 and returned to Saratoga to finish third in the Travers Stakes that summer.

... Saratoga fans are familiar with the "clanging of the bell," which signals the jockeys to weigh out and calls the horses to the paddock. This ritual was conducted at least as early as the 1879 meeting, according to the *Saratogian* of August 7, 1879.

... The Travers Stakes has long been the signature event of Saratoga racing. But it wasn't always so. The Kenner Stakes, for three-year-olds at two miles, carried as much prestige and often exceeded the Travers in value. Luke Blackburn won it in 1880 and earned the richest first prize of that season at $5,925. The Kenner honored Duncan F. Kenner of New Orleans. The millionaire sugar planter and Confederate was devoted to racing and had been president of the Metairie course in Louisiana in the 1830's. He also served as president of the Louisiana Jockey Club.

... Charles Reed, a principal stockholder in the Saratoga Racing Association, conducted yearling sales at his Union Avenue residence during the racing season in the early 1880's.

… A walkover is a stakes race in which there is only one starter, the others declaring themselves out of the event for various reasons. The lone starter must traverse the course to collect the purse and trophy. Walkovers usually involve famous horses, such as Exterminator in the Saratoga Cup of 1921 or Whirlaway in the Pimlico Cup of 1942. Spectacular Bid concluded his career with a walkover in the Woodward at Belmont Park in 1980. At Saratoga in 1899, the Beverwyck Steeplechase was won in a walkover by Dr. Catlett, who earned $1,140 for his effort.

Horse Haven – Contemporary view of the barns and track on the western end of the original track grounds.

Appendix C

STAKES WINNERS OF THE 19TH CENTURY AT SARATOGA RACE COURSE

ADIRONDACK HANDICAP

YEAR	WINNER	DIST.	TIME	OWNER
1889	Princess Bowling	9f	1:57 ½	B. F. Pettit
1890	Rhono	9f	1:56	G. Hearst

ALABAMA STAKES

YEAR	WINNER	DIST.	TIME	OWNER
1872	Woodbine	9f	2:06 ¼	A. Belmont
1873	Minnie W.	9f	2:01 ¾	R. W. Walden
1874	Regardless	9f	2:00 ¼	F. Morris
1875	Olitipa	9f	2:00 ½	A. Belmont
1876	Merciless	9f	2:00 ¾	P. Lorillard
1877	Susquehanna	9f	1:57 ¼	A. Belmont
1878	Belle	9f	1:59	O. Bowie
1879	Ferida	9f	2:00 ¾	G. Lorillard
1880	Glidelia	9f	2:00	W. M. Connor
1881	Thora	9f	1: 59 ¼	C. Reed
1882	Belle of Runnymede	9f	2:08 ¾	Bowen & Co.
1883	Miss Woodford	9f	1:57 ½	Dwyer Bros.

1884	Tolu	9f	2:01	R. W. Walden
1885	Ida Hope	9f	1:59	E. Corrigan
1886	Millie	9f	1:59 ½	Dwyer Bros.
1887	Grisette	9f	2:00 ½	E. J. Baldwin
1888	Bella B.	9f	1:58	Dwyer Bros.
1889	Princess Bowling	9f	2:03 ½	B.F. Pettit
1890	Sinaloa II	9f	1:56 ½	Santa Anita Stable
1891	Sallie McClelland	9f	2:05 ¾	B. McClelland
1892	Ignite	9f	1:57 ½	Bashford Manor
1897	Poetess	9f	2:00 ¼	Wm. Laimbeer

ALBANY HANDICAP

1891	Eon	8f	1:42 ½	P.J. Dwyer & Sons
1892	Saunterer	8f	1:44	W. H. Roller
1893	Loudun	8f	1:45	W.E. Applegate
1894	Clifford	6f	1:13 ¾	Leigh & Rose
1895	Annisette	7f	1:30	P. Lorillard

AMERICAN HOTEL STAKES

1890	Ruperta	8f	1:44	Chicago Stable
1891	La Tosca	8f	1:43 ½	Schuylkill Stable
1892	Stonemell	8f	1:42 ½	H. Warnke

BADEN-BADEN HANDICAP

1880	Elias Lawrence	24f	5:28 ¼	Dwyer Bros.
1881	Thora	24f	5:25 ¼	C. Reed
1882	Lida Stanhope	24f	5:25	J. W. Loud

| 1883 | Gen. Monroe | 24f | 5:36 ¼ | E. J. McElmeel |

BALLSTON HURDLE

| 1893 | Margherita | 16f | 3:56 ¼ | G. R. Tompkins |
| 1894 | Southerner | 16f | 3:53 | J. M. Crosby |

BANKERS STAKES

| 1894 | Franklin | 5f | 1:02 ¼ | J. E. Pepper |
| 1895 | Mussulman | 5f | 1:02 | J. E. Seagram |

BELLE MEADE STAKES

| 1894 | Prince of Monaco | 6f | 1:15 ¼ | C. Fleischmann & Sons |

BEVERWYCK HANDICAP STEEPLECHASE

| 1894 | Woodford | 20f | 6:14 | J. McCabe |

BEVERWYCK STAKES

1887	Volante	*10.4f	2:15 ¾	Santa Anita Stable
1888	Kingston	*10.4f	2:13 ½	Dwyer Bros.
1889	Lavinia Belle	*10.4f	2:12 ½	Beverwyck Stable
1890	Los Angeles	*10.4f	2:13 ¼	Santa Anita Stable
1891	Prince Royal	1 3/16	2:02 ½	P. J. Dwyer & Son
1900	Kinley Mack	8f	1:41	Eastin & Larabie

*Note: The figure 10.4 furlongs used for editing purposes; listed distance is one mile and 500 yards.

BEVERWYCK STEEPLECHASE

1892	Sam Corey	20f	6:19 ½	P. Meaney
1894	Ballarat	20f	6:11	Beverwyck Stable
1895	Sayonara	20f	5:10	W. C. Hayes
1897	Lion Heart	20f	6:09 ½	J. Nixon
1898	Rheinstrom	20f	5:17	F.R.&T. Hitchcock
1899	Dr. Catlett	20f	walkover	J. W. Colt

BITTER ROOT STAKES

1894	Annisette	5f	1:04	Rancocas Stable
1895	Roundsman	6f	1:15	W. C. Hayes

CALIFORNIA STAKES

1887	Royal Arch	8f	1:48	Summit Stable
1888	Kingston	8f	1:44	Dwyer Bros.
1889	Hanover	8f	1:43 ½	Dwyer Bros.
1890	Los Angeles	8f	1:49 ½	Santa Anita Stable
1891	Santiago	8f	1:44	Santa Anita Stable
1894	Necedah	5.5f	1:08 ½	J.E. Pepper

CANADIAN STAKES

1894	Lamplighter	1 3/16	2:04 ¼	G. Walbaum

CASH HANDICAP

1881	Greenland	9f	1:54 ½	G. L. Lorillard
1882	Bootjack	9f	1:54 ¾	M. Young

1883	Brunswick	9f	1:57 ½	Graham Bros.
1884	Lizzie S.	9f	1:59 ½	Graham Bros.
1885	Bettler	9f	1:57 ½	C. W. Mettinger
1886	O'Fallon	9f	1:58	S. S. Brown

CHAMPAGNE HANDICAP

| 1895 | Hazlet | 5.5f | 1:08 ¼ | D. Gideon |
| 1897 | Blueaway | 6f | 1:18 | L. Elmore |

CITIZENS AND MERCHANTS HANDICAP

1897	Ben Brush	10f	2:07 ½	M. F. Dwyer
1899	Swiftmas	1 1/16	1:47	Delmel & Farrell
1900	Charentis	1 1/16	1:45 ½	O. L. Richards

CLARENDON HOTEL STAKES

1879	Bonnie Carrie	10f	2:12	L. Hart
1880	Girofle	10f	2:14 ¼	E. V. Snedeker
1881	Thora	10f	2:11	C. Reed
1882	Francesca	10f	2:14	Dwyer Bros.

CONGRESS HALL STAKES

1879	Bramble	6f	heats	Dwyer Bros.
1880	Oriole	6f	heats	O. Bowie
1881	Bonnie Lizzie	6f	heats	M. Nelson
1882	Bonnie Lizzie	6f	heats	Preakness Stable
1883	Bonnie Lizzie	6f	heats	Preakness Stable

1884	Gleaner	6f	heats	Haydon & Barry
1885	Rapido	6f	heats	E. J. Baldwin
1886	Lady Wayward	6f	heats	J. & J. Swigert
1887	Gleaner	6f	heats	Haydon & Barry
1888	Grisette	6f	heats	Santa Anita Stable
1889	Los Angeles	6f	heats	Santa Anita Stable
1890	Los Angeles	6f	heats	Santa Anita Stable
1891	Los Angeles	6f	1:16 ½	Santa Anita Stable
1892	Lowlander	9f	1:53	F. Lowe
1895	Pennbrook	6f	1:16 ¾	J. E. Kittson
1897	Hamburg	5f	1:02 ½	J. E. Madden

DAY BOAT LINE STAKES

| 1879 | Glidelia | 6f | 1:20 | W. M. Connor |
| 1880 | Thora | 6f | 1:17 ¼ | C. Reed |

DOSWELL STAKES

| 1877 | Cuba | 8f | 1:46 3/5 | E. V. Snedeker |
| 1878 | Perfection | 8f | 1:50 | P. Lorillard |

EQUITY SWEEPSTAKES

1880	Springfield	6f	1:17 ¼	G. W. Darden & Co.
1881	Perplex	6f	1:16 ½	M. Young
1882	Lord Raglan	6f	1:19	N. Armstrong
1883	Lloyd Daly	6f	1:17	W. B. Feland
1884	Ten Stone	6f	1:16 ½	Morris & Patton

1885	Tartar	6f	1:19 ¾	E. Corrigan
1886	Connemara	6f	1:16	Oakwood Stable
1887	Los Angeles	6f	1:17 ¾	Santa Anita Stable
1888	Proctor Knott	6f	1:15 ¾	Bryant & Scoggan
1889	Honduras	6f	1:15 ½	Santa Anita Stable
1890	Cleopatra	6f	1:16 ½	Santa Anita Stable

EXCELSIOR SWEEPSTAKES

1881	Cleopatra	10f	2:08 ½	J. T. Williams
1882	Thora	10f	2:20	C. Reed
1883	Bootjack	10f	2:10	Dwyer Bros.
1884	Freeland	10f	2:11 ½	E. Corrigan
1885	Freeland	10f	2:09	E. Corrigan
1886	Volante	10f	2:13 ½	Santa Anita Stable
1887	Dunbine	10f	2:12 ¼	W. Jennings
1888	Kingston	10f	2:10 ¾	Dwyer Bros.
1889	Los Angeles	10f	2:13	Santa Anita Stable
1890	Los Angeles	10f	2:11 ¾	Santa Anita Stable

FIRST SWEEPSTAKES

| 1886 | Miss Woodford | 8f | 1:43 ¼ | Dwyer Bros. |

FLASH STAKES

1869	Remorseless	4f	:49 ¾	F. Morris
1870	Rattan	4f	:54	M. A. Littell
1871	Nema	4f	:53 ½	Stringfield & Clay

1872	Tom Bowling	4f	:50 ½	H. P. McGrath
1873	Regardless	4f	:50 ½	F. Morris
1874	Olitipa	4f	:47 ¾	Hunter & Travers
1875	Faithless	4f	:49	P. Lorillard
1876	Zoo Zoo	4f	:51 ½	P. Lorillard
1877	Duke of Magenta	4f	:49 ½	G. L. Lorillard
1878	Harold	4f	:49 ¼	G. L. Lorillard
1879	Sensation	4f	:49 ¾	G. L. Lorillard
1880	By The Way	4f	:50 ¾	A. Burnham
1881	Memento	4f	:49 ¾	G. L. Lorillard
1882	George Kenney	4f	:53	Dwyer Bros.
1883	Burton	4f	:49 ¼	Dwyer Bros.
1884	Volante	4f	:49 ½	E. J. Baldwin
1885	Primero	4f	:49 ½	E. J. Baldwin
1886	Agnes	4f	:50 ¾	Dwyer Bros.
1887	King Fish	4f	:50	Dwyer Bros.
1888	Princess Bowling	4f	:50 ½	B. F. Pettit
1889	Protection	4f	:50 ¾	R. E. Campbell
1890	Monterey	4f	:49 ¾	LaBold Bros.
1891	Zorling	4f	:49 ¾	Dwyer & Son
1892	Nick	4f	:49 ¼	Glen Island Stable
1893	Galilee	4f	:49	S. W. Street
1894	Liza	4f	:48	P. Lorillard
1895	Onaretto	4f	:48 ½	W. M. Wallace
1897	Hamburg	4f	:50	J. E. Madden

FLEISCHMANN STAKES

1899	Mesmerist	5.5f	1:07 ½	Bromley & Co.
1900	Bonnibert	5f	1:01 ¼	C. Fleischmann & Sons

FLIRTATION STAKES

1897	Lady Martin	5f	1:02 ½	A. Belmont

FOSTER MEMORIAL

1889	Princess Bowling	1 1/16	1:53 ¾	B. F. Pettit
1890	Ruperta	1 1/16	1:48 ½	B. J. Johnson
1891	Diablo	1 1/8	1:56	Walcott & Campbell
1892	Lowlander	1 1/8	1:53	C. Oxx
1893	Prince Deceiver	1 1/8	1:53 ½	C. R. Jaynes
1894	Yo Tambien	1 1/8	1:54 ¾	Kendall Stable

FOXHALL STAKES

1884	Palinurus	13f	2:54	G. B. Bryson
1885	Bersan	13f	3:00 ½	G. B. Morris
1886	Solid Silver	13f	3:00 ½	Santa Anita Stable
1887	Tramp	13f	2:57	Hurricana Stable
1888	Los Angeles	13f	2:57 ½	Santa Anita Stable
1889	The Lioness	13f	2:54 ¾	McClellan & Roche
1890	Sir John	10f	2:10 ¾	Dwyer Bros.

1891	Pessara	10f	2:13	Walcott & Campbell
1892	Rex	10f	2:18	G. B. Morris
1893	Martyrdom	9f	1:56 ½	J. E. Seagram
1894	Henry of Navarre	9f	1:53 ¾	B. McClelland

GRAND PRIZE OF SARATOGA

1879	Danicheff	14f	3:07	Thos. Puryear & Co.
1880	Luke Blackburn	14f	3:07	Dwyer Bros.
1881	Checkmate	14f	3:01 ¼	J. J. Williams
1882	Glidelia	14f	3:01	W. M. Connor
1883	Meditator	14f	3:04 ½	Dardon & Co.
1884	Gen. Monroe	14f	3:09	E. J. McElmeel
1885	Bob Miles	14f	3:13 ¾	J. J. Williams
1886	Royal Arch	14f	3:09 ¼	Summit Stable
1887	Kaloolah	13f	2:52 ½	J. D. Morrissey
1888	Wary	13f	3:01	T. H. Stevens
1889	Montrose	13f	3:04	Labold Bros.

GRAND UNION HOTEL

1891	Charade	6f	1:16 ½	W. R. Jones
1892	One	6f	1:16 ½	W. H. Timmons
1893	Connors	6f	1:16	C. Smith
1894	Prince of Monaco	5.5f	1:15 ½	C. Fleischmann & Sons

1895	Hazlet	5.5f	1:08 ½	D. Gideon
1897	Archduke	6f	1:15	R. L. Rose
1899	Mesmerist	5.5f	1:08	Bromley & Co.
1900	*Alard Scheck	5f	1:00	J. W. Schorr
	*Far Rockaway	6f	1:14 ¾	J. E. Seagram

*The Grand Union of 1900 was run in two sections, with Alard Scheck winning on Aug. 4 and Far Rockaway winning on Aug. 20.

GRINSTEAD STAKES

1877	Duke of Magenta	6f	1:16 ¾	G. Lorillard
	Spartan (deadheat)			P. Lorillard

HAMBURG STAKES

1898	George Keene	8f	1:47	C. Fleischmann

HARDING STAKES

1877	Zoo Zoo	12f	2:49 ¼	P. Lorillard
1878	Duke of Magenta	12f	2:50 ¾	P. Lorillard

HENDRIE STAKES

1899	May Hempstead	1 1/16	1:48 ½	Headley & Norton
1900	Iroquois Belle	1 1/16	1:49 ¼	A. Featherstone

HOTEL BALMORAL STAKES

1890	Lavinia	12f	2:37	Beverwyck Stable

HUDSON STAKES

| 1892 | False Aherns | 5f | 1:06 | W. H. Timmons |
| 1893 | Buckrene | 5f | 1:04 ¼ | Scoggan Bros. |

HUNTERS STEEPLECHASE

| 1897 | St. Rudolph | 28f | 9:00 | H. W. Smith |

HURRICANA STAKES

1893	Little Matt	5f	1:02	W. B. Jennings
1894	Prince of Monaco	5f	1:01 ¼	C. Fleischmann
1895	Arapahoe	8f	1:42	Santa Anita Stable

IROQUOIS STAKES

1884	Rataplan	10.4f	2:17 ½	N. W. Kittson
1885	Irish Pat	10.4f	2:15 ½	E. Corrigan
1886	Inspector B.	10.4f	2:16 ¼	Dwyer Bros.
1887	Bronzomarte	10.4f	2:17	Excelsior Stable
1888	Pee Weep	10.4f	2:15 ½	W. Hendrie
1889	Flood Tide	10.4f	2:21	Maltese Villa Stable
1890	Sir John	1 1/16	1:51	Dwyer Bros.
1891	Homer	1 1/16	1:52 ½	J. L. Ransdell
1892	Brown Beauty	1 1/16	1:53	H. Stull
1893	Don Fulano	8f	1:48 ¾	Undine Stable
1894	Henry of Navarre	8f	1:43	B. McClelland

KEARNEY STAKES

1887	Eole	12f	2:44 ¾	F. Gebhard
1888	Montrose	12f	2:39	Labold Bros.
1889	Montrose	12f	2:48	Labold Bros.
1890	Los Angeles	12f	2:38	Santa Anita Stable

KENNER STAKES

1870	Enquirer	16f	3:48 ¼	A. Buford
1871	Harry Bassett	16f	3:53 ¾	D. McDaniel
1872	Joe Daniels	16f	3:49	D. McDaniel
1873	Ill Used	16f	3:39	A. Belmont
1874	Stampede	16f	3:42	W. M. Connor
1875	Ozark	16f	3:43 ½	J. M. Harney
	Milner (deadheat)			J. O'Donnell
1876	Charley Howard	16f	3:35	D. McDaniel
1877	Bazil	16f	3:38 ½	P. Lorillard
1878	Duke of Magenta	16f	3:41 ½	P. Lorillard
1879	Falsetto	16f	3:35 ½	W. Hunt Reynolds
1880	Luke Blackburn	16f	3:35 ¼	Dwyer Bros.
1881	Hindoo	16f	3:32	Dwyer Bros.
1882	Boatman	16f	3:34	M. Young
1883	George Kenney	16f	3:38	Dwyer Bros.
1884	Powhatan III	16f	3:36 ½	Churchill & Johnson
1885	Irish Pat	16f	3:45	E. Corrigan
1886	Elkwood	16f	3:34 ¼	W. Gratz

1887	Swarthmore	16f	3:47 ½	Delaware Stable
1888	Los Angeles	16f	3:54 ½	Santa Anita Stable
1889	Long Dance	16f	3:34 ¼	G. M. Rye
1890	English Lady	14f	3:14 ½	Scoggan Bros.
1891	Vallera	14f	3:16 ¼	Scoggan Bros.
1892	Ronald	14f	3:21 ½	C. Fleischmann
1893	Stowaway	10f	2:17	Woodlands Stable
1897	Don De Oro	12f	2:45	A. Belmont

KENSINGTON HURDLE

1900	Dr. Eichberg	16f	4:13 ¼	L. V. Bell

KENSINGTON STAKES

1898	Havoc	8f	1:43 ¼	J. E. Seagram

KENTUCKY STAKES

1870	Harry Bassett	8f	1:51 ¼	D. McDaniel
1871	unnamed filly	8f	1:47 ¾	A. Keene
1872	Silk Stocking	8f	1:52	A. Belmont
1873	Battle Ax	8f	1:45 ½	F. Morris
1874	Chesapeake	8f	1:48 ½	H. P. McGrath
1875	Parole	8f	1:44 ¾	P. Lorillard
1876	Susquehanna	8f	1:45	A. Belmont
1877	Pride of the Village	6f	1:18 ¼	Wm. Astor
1878	Uncas	6f	1:20 ½	P. Lorillard
1879	Oden	6f	1:17 ¾	E. A. Clabaugh

1880	Brambaletta	6f	1:19 ¼	A. Burnham
1881	Onandaga	6f	1:16	Dwyer Bros.
1882	George Kenney	6f	1:15	Dwyer Bros.
1883	Welcher	6f	1:17 ¼	R. W. Walden
1884	Lizzie Dwyer	6f	1:17 ½	E. Corrigan
1885	Quito	6f	1:19 ¼	W. L. Scott
1886	King Fox	6f	1:18	J. B. Haggin
1887	Emperor of Norfolk	6f	1:16	Santa Anita Stable
1888	The Lioness	6f	1:17	Melbourne Stable
1889	Santiago	6f	1:16	Santa Anita Stable
1890	Cleopatra	6f	1:17 ½	Santa Anita Stable
1891	Frank Kinney	6f	1:16	C. R. Jayne
1892	Marguerite	6f	1:15 ¾	J. H. McCormick
1893	Miss Lilly	5.5f	1:09	C. Fleischmann & Sons
1894	Handspun	5.5f	1:11 ¼	Leigh & Rose

LADIES STAKES

1893	Martyrdom	8f	1:42 ¾	J. E. Seagram

LEMP HANDICAP

1899	Maribert	5f	1:02	C. Fleischmann
1900	The Musketeer	5f	1:01 ¾	Mrs. F. Farrell

MADDEN STAKES

1900	Rockton	8f	1:40 ½	Sanford & Sons

McGRATHIANA STAKES

1894	Commoner	5f	1:01	B. McClelland
1895	Diakka	5f	1:02 ¾	P. Lorillard
1899	Mesmerist	5f	1:01 ¼	Bromley & Co.
1900	Lady of the Valley	5f	1:04	R. T. Wilson

MELBOURNE STAKES

1894	Lissak	7f	1:29	Kentucky Stable

MERCHANTS STAKES

1887	Elkwood	13f	heats	W. Gratz
1888	Elkwood	13f	2:50 ½	W. Gratz
1889	Hanover	13f	2:57 ½	Dwyer Bros.
1890	Los Angeles	13f	2:50	Santa Anita Stable
1891	Santiago	12f	2:35 ½	Santa Anita Stable
1892	Dundee	10f	2:09 ½	E. Corrigan
1893	Strathmeath	10f	2:15	G. B. Morris
1894	Lamplighter	9f	1:58 ½	G. Walbaum
1895	Rey El Santa Anita	9f	1:55 ½	Santa Anita Stable

MIDSUMMER HANDICAP

1897	Sir Walter	8f	1:44	Oneck Stable

MISSES STAKES

1881	Tuscaloosa	6f	1:21 ½	L. W. Jerome
1882	Miss Woodford	6f	1:16	Bowen & Co.
1883	Tolu	6f	1:16 ¾	R. W. Walden
1884	Mission Belle	6f	1:16	E. J. Baldwin
1885	Faience	6f	1:18	Preakness Stable
1886	Lizzie Krepps	6f	1:16 ½	S. S. Brown
1887	Geraldine	6f	1:17	Maltese Stable
1889	Mora	6f	1:16 ½	T. H. Stevens
1890	Cleopatra	6f	1:16	Santa Anita Stable
1891	Emma Primrose	6f	1:16 ¼	S. Bryant

MOET & CHANDON STAKES

1894	Clifford	8f	1:40 ½	Leigh & Rose

MONTANA STAKES

1894	Dr. Hasbrouck	8f	1:40 ½	W. M. Barrick

MORRISSEY STAKES

1881	Bushwacker	16f	3:30	G. B. Bryson
1882	Eole	16f	3:42 ½	F. Gebhard
1883	Gen. Monroe	16f	3:33 ½	Yonkers Stable
1884	Gen. Monroe	16f	3:38	J. McElmeel
1885	Freeland	16f	3:42 ½	E. Corrigan
1886	Lucky B.	16f	3:33 ½	Santa Anita Stable
1887	Elkwood	14f	3:08 ½	W. Gratz

1888	Montrose	14f	3:07	Labold Bros.
1889	Lavinia Belle	14f	3:04 ¾	Beverwyck Stable
1890	Flood Tide	14f	3:18	Maltese Villa
1891	Los Angeles	13f	walkover	Santa Anita Stable
1892	Lowlander	1 1/16	1:49 ¾	Ridgewood Stable
1893	Sykeston	1 1/16	1:50 ½	J. B. Dyer
1894	Ducat	8f	1:42 ½	Leigh & Rose

NORTH AMERICAN STEEPLECHASE HANDICAP

1881	Trouble	*22f	5:29	C. Reed
1882	Postguard	*22f	5:20	W. Kavil
1883	Rienzi	*22f	5:14	E. H. Stanley
1884	Beverwyck	*22f	5:31	P. J. Flynn
1885	Major Pickett	*22f	no time taken	
				R. McBride
1886	Bourke Cochran	*22f	5:12	M. N. Nolan
1887	Referee	*22f	5:38 ½	M. T. Danaher
1888	Killarney	*22f	5:22	M. T. Danaher

*Approximate distance

OKALONA STEEPLECHASE

| 1894 | Ballarat | *8 hrd | 4:00 | Beverwyck Stable |
| 1895 | Kilkenny | *8 hrd | 3:53 | T. Welsh |

*Eight hurdles

RANCOCAS STAKES

1895	Victorious	8f	1:43	J. E. Seagram

RELIEF STAKES

1880	Goldbug	13f	2:57	G. B. Morris
1881	Thora	13f	2:51	C. Reed
1882	Carley B.	13f	2:54	A. Burnham
1883	Empress	13f	2:56	O. Bowie
1884	Modesty	13f	2:59	E. Corrigan
1885	Rapido	13f	2:57 ¼	E. J. Baldwin
1886	Mollie McCarty's Last	13f	2:51 ½	E. J. Baldwin
1887	Terra Cotta	13f	2:56 ½	J. W. Guest
1888	Joseph	13f	2:53	E. F. McCarthy
1889	Brown Princess	10.4f	2:11 ½	Beverwyck Stable
1890	Reclare	10.4f	2:22 ½	H. Warnke & Sons

SALVATOR STAKES

1894	Annisette	5.5f	1:08 ¼	P. Lorillard

SARATOGA CUP

1865	Kentucky	18f	4:01 ½	J. Hunter
1866	Kentucky	18f	4:04	J. Hunter
1867	Muggins	18f	4:03	Douglas & Johnson

1868	Lancaster	18f	4:14	M. H. Sanford
1869	Bayonet	18f	4:10	T. G. Moore
1870	Helmbold	18f	4:03 ¾	W. R. Babcock
1871	Longfellow	18f	4:02 ¾	J. Harper
1872	Harry Bassett	18f	3:59	D. McDaniel
1873	Joe Daniels	18f	4:10 ¾	D. McDaniel
1874	Springbok	18f	4:11 ¾	D. McDaniel
1875	Springbok	18f	3:56 ¼	D. McDaniel
	Preakness (deadheat)			M. H. Sanford
1876	Tom Ochiltree	18f	4:06 ½	P. Lorillard
1877	Parole	18f	4:04 ½	P. Lorillard
1878	Parole	18f	4:08 ½	P. Lorillard
1879	Bramble	18f	4:11 ¾	Dwyer Bros.
1880	Long Taw	18f	4:08	G. B. Morris
1881	Checkmate	18f	4:00 ¾	J. T. Williams
1882	Thora	18f	4:05 ½	C. Reed
1883	Gen. Monroe	18f	4:21 ½	Yonkers Stable
1884	Gen. Monroe	18f	4:05	E. J. McElmeel
1885	Bob Miles	18f	4:02	J. T. Williams
1886	Volante	18f	4:25	Santa Anita Stable
1891	Los Angeles	16f	3:43 ½	Santa Anita Stable

SARATOGA GRAND PRIZE

1899	Don De Oro	9f	2:00 ½	J. Boden

SARATOGA GREEN STEEPLECHASE
1897   Royal Scarlet   20f   6:33   F.R.&T. Hitchcock

SARATOGA HUNT CUP STEEPLECHASE
1900   Diver   20f   6:32 ½   E. L. Smith

SARATOGA PINK COAT STEEPLECHASE
1897   Trillion   28f   8:36   W. C. Hayes

SARATOGA PRIZE
1895   Rey El Santa Anita 8f   1:43 ¼   Santa Anita Stable

SARATOGA STAKES
1864   Saratoga   8f   2:08 ½   J. Hunter
1865   Ulrica   8f   1:51 ¼   J. Hunter
1866   Red Wing   8f   1:51 ½   P. C. Bush
1867   Relentless   6f   1:20   F. Morris
1868   *Oakleaf   6f   1:19 ¼   D. McDaniel
1869   Remorseless   6f   1:18 ¼   F. Morris
1870   Mary Louise   6f   1:18 ½   J. O' Donnell
1871   St. Patrick   6f   1:20   F. Morris
1872   Catesby   6f   1:17 ½   O. Bowie
1873   Steel Eyes   6f   1:22 ½   A. Belmont
1874   Willie Burke 6f   1:23 ¾   D. McDaniel
1875   Parole   6f   1:18 ¾   P. Lorillard
1876   Leonard   6f   1:17 ½   H. P. McGrath

1877	Bramble	6f	1:17 ½	Johnson & Co.
1878	Harold	6f	1:20	G. L. Lorillard
1879	Sensation	6f	1:18	G. L. Lorillard
1880	Crickmore	6f	1:17 ¼	O. Bowie
1881	Vanguard	6f	1:15 ¾	G. L. Lorillard
1882	George Kenney	6f	1:16 ½	Dwyer Bros.
1883	Panique	6f	1:17 ¼	N. W. Kittson
1884	Lizzie Dwyer	6f	1:18 ½	E. Corrigan
1885	Ban Fox	6f	1:16 ½	B. A. Haggin
1886	King Fox	6f	1:16	J. B. Haggin
1887	Emperor of Norfolk	6f	1:17	Santa Anita Stable
1888	Gipsy Queen	6f	1:16	Excelsior Stable
1889	Honduras	6f	1:18 ½	Santa Anita Stable
1890	Balgowan	6f	1:17	T. J. Clay
1891	Miss Dixie	5f	1:04	J. E. Pepper
1892	Foraker	5f	1:03	C. Fleischmann
1893	William T.	5f	1:01 ¼	May & Hall

*Note: Oakleaf deadheated with an unnamed filly owned by Francis Morris. Oakleaf then won in a runoff in 1:21 ¾.

SARATOGA STEEPLCHASE

1900	Trillion	20f	6:16 ½	W. C. Hayes

SEA FOAM STAKES

1893	Racine	5.5f	1:07 ½	Undine Stable
1894	Clifford	5.5f	1:07 ¼	Leigh & Rose

SEQUEL STAKES

1864	Kentucky	16f	3:37 ½	J. Hunter
1865	Baltimore	16f	3:43 ½	Bowie & Hall
1866	Stonewall Jackson	16f	3:41	T. G. Moore
1867	Ruthless	16f	3:37 ½	F. Morris
1868	Gen. Duke	16f	3:40 ¾	McConnell & Harness
1869	Narragansett	16f	3:37 ¾	Dennison & Crawford
1870	Maggie B.	16f	3:37 ¼	M. A. Littell
1871	Mary Clark	16f	3:40	M. A. Littell
1872	Wade Hampton	16f	3:42 ½	A. Belmont
1873	Ill Used	16f	3:40 ½	A. Belmont
1874	Vandalite	16f	3:40 ¾	A. B. Lewis & Co.
1875	Viator	16f	3:43 ¼	E. A. Clabaugh
1876	Parole	14f	3:10 ¾	P. Lorillard
1877	Zoo Zoo	14f	3:10	P. Lorillard
1878	Duke of Magenta	14f	3:15	G. L. Lorillard
1879	Rochester	14f	3:13 ¼	E. A. Clabaugh
1880	Ferncliffe	14f	3:09 ¾	Babcock & Co.
1881	Hindoo	14f	3:21	Dwyer Bros.
1882	Boatman	14f	3:05 ½	M. Young
1883	Drake Carter	13f	2:53 ½	Morris & Patton
1884	Modesty	13f	2:56	E. Corrigan
1885	Volante	13f	3:00	E. J. Baldwin
1886	Elkwood	13f	2:54 ½	W. Gratz

SPENCER HANDICAP

1891	Pessara	10f	2:10	Walcott & Campbell
1892	Badge	10f	2:07	J. Mullins
1893	Strathmeath	10f	2:12 ¾	G. B. Morris
1894	Yo Tambien	10f	2:07 ¼	Kendall Stable
1895	Sir Excess	10f	2:08 ½	J. W. Rogers
1897	Flying Dutchman	10f	2:10	P. Dunne
1898	Poetess	10f	2:07 ¼	Wm. Laimbeer
1899	Laverok	10f	2:06 ½	Wm. Hendrie
1900	Martimas	9f	1:53 ½	Wm. Hendrie

SPINAWAY STAKES

1881	Memento	5f	1:06	G. L. Lorillard
1882	Miss Woodford	5f	1:03 ½	Bowen & Co.
1883	Tolu	5f	1:03 ¾	R. W. Walden
1884	Mission Belle	5f	1:03	E. J. Baldwin
1885	Biggonet	5f	1:05	W. P. Burch
1886	Grisette	5f	1:03 ¼	E. J. Baldwin
1887	Los Angeles	5f	1:02 ½	E. J. Baldwin
1888	Gipsy Queen	5f	1:03	Excelsior Stable
1889	Daisy F.	5f	1:06 ¼	H. B. Durham
1890	Sallie McClelland	5f	1:06	B. McClelland
1891	Promenade	5f	1:03	LaBold Bros.

SPIRIT OF THE TIMES STAKES

1891   Forerunner   8.5f   1:49 ¼   E. Brown

SPORTSMAN STAKES

1891   Forerunner   9f   2:03 ¼   E. Brown

SPRINGBOK STAKES

1893   Appomatox   5f   1:02   J. B. Dyer

SUMMER HANDICAP

Year	Horse	Distance	Time	Owner
1870	Nannie Douglas	18f	4:28 ½	Bacon & Holland
1871	Hamburg	18f	4:01 ¾	T. Page
1872	Defender	18f	4:24 ½	J. Morrissey
1873	Strachino	16f	3:36 ¾	Hunter & Travers
1874	Lizzie Lucas	16f	3:39 ½	J. Donahue
1875	Grinstead	16f	3:37 ½	T. Puryear & Co.
1876	Vigil	14f	3:07 ¼	D. McDaniel
1877	Parole	14f	3:08	P. Lorillard
1878	Loulanier	14f	3:14	G. Lorillard
1879	Franklin	12f	2:39 ½	J. Bell
1880	Luke Blackburn	12f	2:39	Dwyer Bros.
1881	Checkmate	12f	2:35 ¼	J. T. Williams
1882	Bend Or	12f	2:35 ½	Churchill & Co.
1883	Ella Warfield	12f	2:39 ½	Davis & Hall
1884	Referee	12f	2:42 ½	W. L. Scott
1885	Euclid	12f	2:41 ½	Preakness Stable
1886	Royal Arch	12f	2:39 ½	Summit Stable

TENNESSEE HANDICAP

1881	Tuscaloosa	6f	1:16	L. W. Jerome
1882	George Kinney	6f	1:15	Dwyer Bros.
1883	Welcher	6f	1:18 ¼	R. W. Walden
1884	Telie Doe	6f	1:16	W. P. Burch
1885	Kirkman	6f	1:17	W. L. Cassidy
1886	Connemara	6f	1:17 ¾	Oakwood Stable
1887	Emperor of Norfolk	6f	1:19 ¼	Santa Anita Stable
1888	Gipsy Queen	6f	1:16 ½	Excelsior Stable
1889	Eberlee	6f	1:16	J. K. Megibben & Co.
1890	Monterey	6f	1:16 ¾	Labold Bros.

TEST STAKES

1891	Charade	7f	1:31	W. R. Jones

TRAVERS STAKES

1864	Kentucky	14f	3:18 ¾	J. Hunter
1865	Maiden	14f	3:18 ½	T. G. Moore
1866	Merrill	14f	3:29	R. A. Alexander
1867	Ruthless	14f	3:13 ¼	F. Morris
1868	The Banshee	14f	3:10 ¾	J. M. Clay
1869	Glenelg	14f	3:14	A. Belmont
1870	Kingfisher	14f	3:15 ¼	D. Swigert
1871	Harry Bassett	14f	3:21 ½	D. McDaniel

1872	Joe Daniels	14f	3:08 ¼	D. McDaniel
1873	Tom Bowling	14f	3:09 ¾	H. P. McGrath
1874	*Attila	14f	3:08 ¾	P. Lorillard
1875	D'Artagnan	14f	3:06 ½	J. A. Grinstead
1876	Sultana	14f	3:15 ½	A. Belmont
1877	Baden Baden	14f	3:12 ¼	W. Astor
1878	Duke of Magenta	14f	3:08	G. Lorillard
1879	Falsetto	14f	3:09 ¼	J. W. Reynolds
1880	Grenada	14f	3:12 ½	G. Lorillard
1881	Hindoo	14f	3:07 ½	Dwyer Bros.
1882	Carley B.	14f	3:28 ¾	A. Burnham
1883	Barnes	14f	3:18	Dwyer Bros.
1884	Rataplan	14f	3:07 ½	N. W. Kittson
1885	Bersan	14f	3:08 ¼	G. B. Morris
1886	Inspector B.	14f	3:10 ¼	Dwyer Bros.
1887	Carey	14f	3:17 ½	E. Corrigan
1888	Sir Dixon	14f	3:07 ¾	Dwyer Bros.
1889	Long Dance	14f	3:08 ¾	G. M. Rye
1890	Sir John	12f	2:39	Dwyer Bros.
1891	Vallera	12f	2:49	Scoggan Bros.
1892	Azra	12f	2:43 ¾	Bashford Manor
1893	Stowaway	10f	2:10 ¾	Woodland Stable
1894	Henry of Navarre	10f	2:10 ¼	B. McClelland
1895	Liza	9f	1:55 ½	P. Lorillard
1897	Rensselaer	10f	2:12	J. E. McDonald

*Attila and Acrobat finished in a deadheat in 3:09 ½. The judges called for a race-off, which Attila won in 3:08 ¾.

TRENTON STAKES

1892　False Aherns　5f　1:03 ½　W. H. Timmons

TROUBLE STEEPLECHASE

1881	Trouble	22f	5:56 ½	C. Reed
1882	Postguard	22f	5:23	W. Karit
1883	Postguard	18f	4:24 ½	W. Karit
1884	Rienzi	18f	4:29	E. H. Stanley
1885	Quebec	18f	4:29	Excelsior Stable
1886	Bourke Cochran	18f	4:23	M. N. Nolan
1887	Wheatly	18f	4:27	Morris & Harwood
1888	Monte Christo	18f	4:45	Queens Co. Stable

TROY STAKES

1891	Eon	6.5f	1:25	Dwyer & Son
1892	Stonenell	6f	1:14	H. Warnke

TURF FIELD AND FARM STAKES

1891　Foreigner　6f　1:20　E. Brown

UNITED STATES HOTEL STAKES

1879	Volturno	12f	2:41 ¼	S. Powers & Sons
1880	Luke Blackburn	12f	2:41	Dwyer Bros.
1881	Hindoo	12f	2:36	Dwyer Bros.
1882	Frankie B.	12f	2:40 ½	A. Burnham

1883	Drake Carter	12f	2:36	Morris & Co.
1884	Kosciusko	12f	2:40 ½	Haydon & Barry
1885	Favor	12f	2:40	Morris & Patton
1886	Inspector B.	12f	2:42 ¾	Dwyer Bros.
1887	Hanover	12f	2:38 ½	Dwyer Bros.
1888	Ballston	12f	2:40	Chickasaw Stable
1889	Retrieve	12f	2:38 ½	Labold Bros.
1890	Sinaloa II	12f	2:37 ½	Santa Anita Stable
1891	Bermuda	12f	2:39	B. McClelland
1892	Copyright	9f	1:56 ½	Baden Stable
1893	Deception	9f	1:55 ¼	J. McDermott
1894	Peacemaker	7f	1:29	Goughacres Stable
1895	Axiom	5f	1:02 ¾	P. J. Dwyer
1897	Braw Lad	8f	1:45 ½	H. Stull
1898	George Keene	9f	1:57	C. Fleischmann
1899	Kinley Mack	9f	1:54 ¾	Eastin & Larabie

VAN TASSEL & KEARNEY STEEPLECHASE

1894	Ballarat	*8 hrd	4:01	Beverwyck Stable

*Eight hurdles

VIRGINIA STAKES

1881	Runnymede	6f	1:15 ½	Dwyer Bros.
1882	Barnes	6f	1:15	Bowen & Co.
1883	Burton	5f	1:03 ¾	Dwyer Bros.
1884	Lizzie Dwyer	5f	1:04	E. Corrigan

1885	Kirkman	5f	1:03 ¾	W. L. Cassidy
1886	Laredo	5f	1:02 ¾	Santa Anita Stable
1887	Emperor of Norfolk	5f	1:03 ½	Santa Anita Stable
1888	Caliente	5f	1:03	Santa Anita Stable
1889	Gun Wad	5f	1:06 ½	A. J. Scott
1890	Palestine	5f	1:02 ¾	W. H. Laudeman

WATKINS STAKES

1892	One	5f	1:04 ½	W. H. Timmons

WELTER STAKES

1882	Bend Or	8f	1:45	Churchill & Co.
1883	Navarro	8f	1:45 ¾	Yonkers Stable

WINDSOR HOTEL STAKES

1879	Grenada	5f	1:03 ½	G. L. Lorillard
1880	Crickmore	5f	1:05	O. Bowie

WORDEN HOUSE STAKES

1895	Florrie	4.5f	:48 ½	G. Walbaum
1897	Highjinks	5f	1:02 ¾	W. M. Wallace
1899	Flower of Gold	5f	1:01 ½	W. B. Jennings
1900	Manga	5f	1:01	Ms. M. Oliver

CHRONOLOGY OF NOTEWORTHY EVENTS

August 3, 1863.   Opening day of inaugural thoroughbred race meeting in Saratoga Springs.

August 2, 1864.   First edition of the Travers Stakes, won by Kentucky. Hurdle race on the last day of this meeting.

August 8, 1865.   First edition of the Saratoga Cup, won by Kentucky.

August 7, 1867.   The filly Ruthless, who earlier this year won the inaugural Belmont Stakes, won the Travers Stakes.

August 9, 1868.   The Preakness Stakes, second leg of the Triple Crown, is conceived by racing leaders in Saratoga Springs.

August 4, 1869.   First edition of the Flash Stakes, won by
                   Remorseless, a full sister to Ruthless.

July, 1870.   The Saratoga Racing Association begins
                   an era of two annual summer meetings
                   in Saratoga Springs.

July, 1872.   John Morrissey introduces pari-mutuel
                   betting at this meeting, based on the
                   French system of "Paris Mutuels."

July 16, 1872.   Harry Bassett defeats Longfellow and
                   Defender in the Saratoga Cup.

July 19, 1872.   First edition of the Alabama Stakes, won
                   by Woodbine.

May 1, 1878.   Death of John Morrissey.

July 20, 1878.   Duke of Magenta won the Travers
                   Stakes.

July 28, 1881.   First edition of the Spinaway Stakes, won
                   by Memento.

July, August, 1882.   Longest Saratoga meeting of the 19th century at 40 days.

August 4, 1887.   Emperor of Norfolk won the Saratoga Stakes, his first of four Saratoga stakes wins within 15 days.

November, 1891.   Gottfried Walbaum and partners purchase Saratoga Race Course.

July 23, 1894.   Henry of Navarre won the Travers Stakes.

July, August, 1895.   The meeting is cut short from a scheduled 40 days to 28 days.

July 28, 1897.   Racing returns after a one-year absence in 1896. Hamburg wins the Flash Stakes.

November, 1900.   William C. Whitney leads a syndicate which purchases the track from Walbaum.

NOTES

1. FOUNDATIONS 1863-1869

1. Landon Manning, *The Noble Animals* (Saratoga Springs, NY: n.p., 1973), 27-28.

2. John Hervey, *Racing in America, 1665-1865*, vol. 2 (New York: The Jockey Club and Scribner Press, 1944), 339-340.

3. *New York Times*, 1 August 1863.

4. *Spirit of the Times*, 9 October 1847.

5. W. S. Vosburgh, *Racing in America, 1866-1921* (New York: The Jockey Club), 7.

6. *Republican and Sentinel*, 12 August 1864.

7. *New York Times*, 2 August 1866.

8. *New York Times*, 11 August 1868.

9. *Laurel-Pimlico Media Guide 2000* (n.p.: Maryland Jockey Club, 2000), 7, 60.

2. EXPANSION AND CHALLENGE 1870-1890

1. *New York Times*, 15 July 1871.

2. *Fair Grounds Race Course 1999-2000 Record &*
    Information Guide (n.p.: Fair Grounds Race
    Course, n.d.), 10.

3. *Saratogian*, 7 August 1879.

4. H. G. Crickmore, (New York: n.p., n.d.), n.p.

5. 23 July 1881.

6. *New York Times*, 16 July 1882.

7. *New York Times*, 9 July 1883.

8. Tracy Gantz, "Racing in the West: The Early Days,"
    Daily Racing Form, 2 November, 1996

3. DECLINE AND RECOVERY 1891-1900

1. "The Unruly Reign of Gottfried Walbaum," research project by Andy Radloff compiled from Gottfried Walbaum memoirs, property of Frank Tannehill, Jr., *National Museum of Racing and Hall of Fame Quarterly*, Summer 1999, 8.

2. Hugh Bradley, *Such Was Saratoga* (New York: Doubleday, Doran and Co., Inc., 1940), 209.

3. *New York Times*, 10 August 1893.

4. *Goodwin's Turf Guide* (New York: Goodwin Bros., 1893).

5. *New York Times*, 16 August 1894.

6. *Saratogian*, 7 July 1994.

7. Bradley, 227-231.

8. *New York Times*, 20 August 1897.

9. *New York Times*, 26 August 1900.

10. *New York Times*, 2 November 1900.

11. Joseph Freeman Marster, *Mansey's Magazine*, November 1902, 161-171.

12. Mark D. Hirsh, *William C. Whitney – Modern Warlock* (New York: Dodd, Mead and Co., 1948), 589-590.

13. Dan Bowmar, *Giants of the Turf* (Lexington, KY: The Blood-Horse, n.d.), 177.

14. *Saratogian*, 21 August 1902.

15. *New York Times*, 5 August 1901.

16. *Saratogian*, 23 October 1911, 10 July 1912.

SELECTED BIBLIOGRAPHY

BOOKS

The American Racing Manual 1945-2000. New York: Daily Racing Form, n.d.

The American Racing Record and Turf Guide, 1870-1872. New York: W.G. Dorling, n.d.

The American Turf. New York: The Historical Co., 1898.

Bowmar, Dan M. *Giants of the Turf.* Lexington, KY: The Blood-Horse, n.d.

Bradley, Hugh. *Such Was Saratoga.* New York: Doubleday, Doran and Co., Inc., 1940.

Britten, Evelyn Barrett. *Chronicles of Saratoga.* Saratoga Springs, NY: Bradshaw Printing Co., 1947.

Gardiner, Alexander. *Canfield.* Garden City, NY: Doubleday, Doran and Co., Inc., 1930.

Hervey, John. *Racing in America, 1665-1865*. Vol. 2. New York: The Jockey Club and Scribner Press, 1944.

Hirsch, Mark D. *William C. Whitney – Modern Warlock*. New York: Dodd, Mead and Co., 1948.

Horses in the National Museum of Racing Hall of Fame. Compiled by the National Turf Writers Association. Saratoga Springs, NY: National Museum of Racing, n.d.

Hotaling, Edward. *They're Off – Horse Racing at Saratoga*. Syracuse, NY: Syracuse University Press, 1995.

Manning, Landon. *The Noble Animals*. Saratoga Springs, NY: N.p., 1973.

New York Racing Association. *New York Racing Association Media Guide 2002*. New York: New York Racing Association, 2002.

New York Racing Laws and Reports, 1897-1905. N.p., n.d.

Strong, Phil. *Horses and Americans*. New York: Frederick A. Stokes Co., 1939.

Trevathan, Charles E. *The American Thoroughbred*. New York: Macmillan & Co., 1905.

Vosburgh, W. S. *Racing in America, 1866-1921*. New York: The Jockey Club, 1922.

Waller, George. *Saratoga: Saga of an Impious Era*. Englewood Cliffs, NJ: Prentice-Hall, 1966.

ANNUAL PUBLICATIONS AND CALENDARS

The American Jockey Club Racing Calendar, 1874. N.p.: The American Jockey Club, n.d.

The American Racing Record and Turf Guide, 1870-1871. New York: W. G. Doring, n.d.

The American Racing Record and Turf Guide, 1872. New York : W. G. Doring, n.d.

The American Racing Record and Turf Guide, 1873-1874. New York : W. G. Doring, n.d.

The American Turf Register, 1874. New York: Turf, Field and Farm, n.d.

Goodwin's Turf Guide 1888. New York: Goodwin Bros., 1888.

Goodwin's Turf Guide 1889. New York: Goodwin Bros., 1889.

Goodwin's Turf Guide 1890. New York: Goodwin Bros., 1890.

Goodwin's Turf Guide 1891. New York: Goodwin Bros., 1891.

Goodwin's Turf Guide 1892. New York: Goodwin Bros., 1892.

Goodwin's Turf Guide 1893. New York: Goodwin Bros., 1893.

Goodwin's Turf Guide 1894. New York: Goodwin Bros., 1894.

Goodwin's Turf Guide 1895. New York: Goodwin Bros., 1895.

Goodwin's Turf Guide 1896. New York: Goodwin Bros., 1896.

Goodwin's Turf Guide 1897. New York: Goodwin Bros., 1897.

Goodwin's Turf Guide 1898. New York: Goodwin Bros., 1898.

Goodwin's Turf Guide 1899. New York: Goodwin Bros., 1899.

Goodwin's Turf Guide 1900. New York: Goodwin Bros., 1900.

Laurel-Pimlico Media Guide 2000. N.p.: Maryland Jockey Club, 2000.

PERIODICALS, JOURNALS AND UNPUBLISHED PAPERS

Clarkin, Franklin. *Harper's Weekly*, 31 August 1901.

Goldman, Davis I. "Longfellow." *Saratoga Summer Magazine,* Summer 1991, 61-65.

Hoffman, Robert V. "Saratoga, Here They Come!" *Country Life* 60 (August 1931): 35-37.

Marster, Joseph Freeman. *Mansey's Magazine*, November 1902.

Nash, Richard. "Big Red Machine." *The Blood-Horse*, 3 March 2001.

Newman, Neil. "Saratoga – Its Fall and Rise." *The National Turf Digest*, September 1930.

Radloff, Andy. "The Unruly Reign of Gottfried Walbaum." *National Museum of Racing and Hall of Fame Quarterly*, Summer 1999.

Radloff, Andy. "The Unruly Reign of Gottfried Walbaum." *National Museum of Racing and Hall of Fame Quarterly,* Fall 1999.

Smith, Carol Chandler. "Splendid Survivors: Horse Racing Stables Construction, Saratoga Springs, New York 1840-1913." Thesis presented to the Faculty of the Graduate School of Cornell University, Ithaca, NY, 1987.

Veitch, Michael. "Ruthless: New York Champion of the 1860's." *New York Thoroughbred*, May 1992.

NEWSPAPERS

Daily America (New York) 17 August 1902.

Daily Racing Form (Hightstown, NJ) 23 July 1895, 5 December 1987, 2 November 1996.

New York Times 1863-1901.

Republican and Sentinel (Saratoga Springs, NY) July/August 1864.

Saratoga Union (Saratoga Springs, NY) 1887.

Saratogian (Saratoga Springs, NY) 1872-1901.

Spirit of the Times (New York) 9 October 1847, 23 July 1881.

ACKNOWLEDGEMENTS
AND CREDITS

I am grateful to all who provided help and support for this study. My wife Gail and our five children kept encouraging me to stick with the often tedious research in bringing together this picture of early Saratoga racing.

At the start, Ellen De Lalla and Jean Stamm of the Saratoga Public Library were very helpful with the resources of the Saratoga Room. I am also appreciative of the beautiful setting and tranquility provided by the Feinberg Library at Plattsburgh State University.

The editor of this work is Gale Y. Brinkman, a teacher of English whose professional guidance was central to the organization and presentation of this work.

Many thanks go to the proofreaders for their time and suggestions. My father Don, whose own father and grandfather were talented horsemen at North American tracks from the 1880's to the 1920's, helped out with his knowledge of Saratoga Springs as a lifelong racing fan. Few people have a better knowledge of Saratoga Race Course than George Hathaway, the resident manager of the track for the New York Racing Association.

I sincerely appreciate the help of Jane Schwartz, author of *Ruffian, Burning From The Start,* for giving her time, as well as that of Mark Cusano, a friend and keen observer of the racing scene.

Tom Gilcoyne, the indefatigable researcher for the National Museum of Racing and Hall of Fame, and Richard Hamilton, the Museum's Communications Director, both made many important observations and corrections during their review. I would also like to thank Beth Sheffer, the Collections Manager for the Museum, for her time with this project.

My thanks also go to Eclipse Award winning photographer Barbara D. Livingston, whose photographs of the track appear in this book. Barbara is the author of *Old Friends*, a photographic essay of famous and not-so-famous thoroughbreds in her life, and of *Four Seasons,* a seasonal review of North American racing.

The photos on the front and back cover, and the contemporary Horse Haven scene on page 60 are by Livingston. Ruthless, on page 15, and Duke of Magenta, on page 28, are provided courtesy of the National Museum of Racing. The photo of William C. Whitney on page 48, by Bert Morgan, is from the collection of the author.

The emblem that appears throughout this book is a reproduction of a stable admission badge for the 1882 season at Saratoga Race Course.

– NOTES –

– NOTES –